Critical Thinking in Business

Revised & expanded

2nd Edition

Bob Schoenberg

Heuristic Books

Saint Charles, Missouri USA

Copyright Notice:

ISBN 978-1-59630-097-2
LCCN 2015937002

Library of Congress Cataloging-in-Publication Data from the first edition:
Schoenberg, Bob.
  Critical thinking in business / Bob Schoenberg.
    p. cm.
  Includes bibliographical references.
  ISBN 978-1-59630-024-8 (alk. paper)
  1. Decision making. 2. Problem solving. 3. Organizational effectiveness. 4. Success in business. 5. Critical thinking.
    I. Title.
  HD30.23.S373 2007
  658.4'03--dc22

                                        2007017484

Heuristic Books
is an imprint of

𝕾𝖈𝖎𝖊𝖓𝖈𝖊 & 𝕳𝖚𝖒𝖆𝖓𝖎𝖙𝖎𝖊𝖘 𝕻𝖗𝖊𝖘𝖘
Saint CharlesMO 63301-6571
636-394-4950
Heuristicbooks.com

Heuristic Books
for Mathematics & Management Science
heuristicbooks.com

Second Edition Changes

What's different in this second edition of Critical Thinking in Business?

Additional Exercises – each chapter has been expanded and includes more practice exercises. It is like having a workbook with a book.

Appendix – at the back of the book is an appendix with an answer key containing many, but not all of the answers. Due to the nature of critical thinking, it is not possible to list all of the possible correct answers. Therefore, not every answer will be found. However, if you get stumped, you're likely to find the answer in the Appendix.

New Chapter – an entirely new chapter entitled: "Critical Thinking and Social Media" has been included. This chapter highlights a number of issues associated with social media and show you how to apply various critical thinking skills to develop your strategy and policy regarding social media.

Final Summary – the last chapter lists all the critical thinking skills discussed and provides a definition for each one. This is a handy summary of the critical thinking skills discussed in the entire book.

Contact information on how to reach the author has been updated.

Acknowledgements

There are several people I'd like to thank for helping to make this book possible. First, I'd like to thank Alan Olinsky for inspiring me to write this book. It was Alan who initially suggested that I write this book and encouraged me to do so.

Next, I'd like to thank Allyn Bradford who provided continuous support and encouragement. Allyn also wrote the Foreword of this book.

Finally, I'd like to thank my publisher, Bud Banis, for his faith in me, and for bringing this work to fruition.

Dedication

In memory of Leonard Schoenberg,
my beloved father

Foreword:

This book is a straightforward guide on how to make successful business decisions. It gives you the tools to sort out your own thinking so you can really get what you want, whether you are buying or selling, instead of making impulsive decisions that you might later regret.

Bob Schoenberg is an old friend of mine. We are also colleagues in the department of Critical and Creative Thinking at U-Mass, Boston. In a sense we are online colleagues, in that we both teach online courses at that university and almost all of our contact with each other is over the net as well.

In this book, and I know there will be others, Bob shares with us his practicable wisdom about how to survive in the marketplace. He knows both the business world and Critical Thinking well enough to mesh the two into a handy way to make wise business decisions... Everyone needs to know about these things. This knowledge is especially useful when you are out shopping for a house, a car or any anything else.

I know you will enjoy this book; but more than that, you will enjoy the results of making wise business decisions.

J. Allyn Bradford   *Cambridge, Massachusetts*

TABLE OF CONTENTS

Introduction

This book provides a number of critical thinking skills for people who work in the business world. When I first began teaching an online graduate course in Critical Thinking for UMASS at Boston, most of my students were education majors. However, gradually I've gotten more business students and began including more business applications in the curriculum. As I began researching the field of critical thinking in business, I discovered that while there were a number of business schools that recognize the importance of critical thinking, few if any offer a specific course in critical thinking. Faculty members are experts in their respective fields: accounting, finance, management, marketing, sales, etc. But critical thinking, although interdisciplinary, is not specifically a business skill. Yet, successful business people do use critical thinking.

Recognizing a need for critical thinking in business, I decided to write this book. Being an entrepreneur myself and having obtained a Masters in Critical and Creative Thinking from UMASS at Boston, I've attempted to bridge the gap between critical thinking and business. However, it was the gradual increase in business students attending my class on Critical Thinking that really motivated me to make this connection.

Essentially, I have highlighted several critical thinking skills, explained what they are, how to do them and specifically how to use them in a business setting. Each chapter focuses upon a different critical thinking skill.

Chapter One explains what critical thinking is. I provide several different definitions including one of my own.

Chapter Two describes how assumptions can be dangerous, especially in a work setting. I describe the different types of assumptions – value assumptions, reality assumptions and how assumptions have an impact on decision making, often raising havoc in the business world.

Chapter Three on Frames of Reference provides an in depth look at how this critical thinking skill is used in marketing and sales. I also explain how identifying a person's frame of reference is not only a tremendous sales aide, but also can be very useful in negotiations.

Chapter Four emphasizes the importance of asking questions. I provide several different categories of questions.

Chapter Five examines the importance of causal relationships. In this chapter I extrapolate formal logic and bring it into the practical realm and show how it can be used in a work setting.

Chapter Six explains Methodological Believing. In this chapter I explain how this unique type of role play can be used in a business setting and why it would be useful and beneficial to use it.

Chapter Seven explores the relationship between Stress and Critical Thinking and documents the necessity of managing stress to promote critical thinking. Several specific methods for reducing stress are presented.

Chapter Eight delves into the world of Ethics. In recent years, many corporations have come under scrutiny and their ethics have been called into question. In this chapter I provide several "tests" to help you become clear about your ethics and beliefs.

Chapter Nine explains how to apply critical thinking skills in social media.

Chapter ten ties everything together and summarizes all the various critical thinking skills covered in this book.

Definitions of Critical Thinking

There are probably over 100 definitions of Critical Thinking. I've been teaching graduate courses in Critical Thinking for several years and each semester I ask my students to create their own definition of Critical Thinking. Each one of them does and their definitions are all valid. You can find definitions ranging from a few words to a few paragraphs. I've included a few in this chapter.

My definition of Critical Thinking keeps changing. However, when I'm asked the question, "What is Critical Thinking?", (which is a question I'm frequently asked), my response is: Critical thinking is a set of higher order thinking skills that include: metacognition (thinking about your thinking), frames of reference, seeking evidence and other skills, which will be discussed later. By higher order thinking skills, I mean that a higher level of thinking- thinking beyond the ordinary level is required. Critical means important or urgent.

This is a special type of thinking that can be used for important decision making, when seeking evidence, clarifying information and a variety of other situations that require more than the usual type of thinking that people use.

Suppose for example, you are deciding what to have for dinner. That wouldn't require you to think critically. However, if you were planning a dinner for a party of 20 people and some of them had various types of food allergies, you'd probably need to think critically to determine what food to serve. Once you knew what foods certain people couldn't eat, you'd probably need to think critically to determine what food to serve. This is not as simple as it seems, because food manufacturers don't always list everything that's in the food. Remember, Critical Thinking also involves seeking evidence. Would it be sufficient to call a food manufacturer and rely upon what you were told by a customer service person?

How do you know if this person has the proper knowledge and training to answer your question correctly? If this person gives you the wrong information, some of you dinner guests could end up sick or even dead! I think you can begin to see that Critical thinking has much more depth to it than ordinary thinking.

Here are what some other authors have to say about Critical Thinking. Paul (1990) states that Critical Thinking is "Disciplined, self-directed thinking which exemplifies the perfections of thinking appropriate to a particular mode or domain of thinking (p554). He also describes critical thinking as "Thinking that displays mastery of intellectual skills and abilities " (p55).

The following information is from Tim Van Gelder's website on Critical Thinking on the Web at (http://www.austhink.org/critical/pages/definitions.html):

Ennis (1989) describes critical thinking as "reasonable reflective thinking that is focused on deciding what to do or believe" (Alec Fisher PDF file (http://www.austhink.org/critical/pages/definitions.html).

Fisher and Scriven (1997, p.21):

Critical thinking is the skilled and active interpretation and evaluation of observations and communications, information and argumentation.

Nickerson, Perkins and Smith (1985):

The ability to judge the plausibility of specific assertions, to weigh evidence, to assess the logical soundness of inferences, to construct counter-arguments and alternative hypotheses.

Now that you have a better understanding of what Critical Thinking is, you may be wondering how it is used in business. The remaining chapters in this book explain that. It's important to realize that critical thinking skills are not limited exclusively for people in the business world. These skills can be used in many professions and even in your personal life. However, the focus of this book is on critical thinking in business. So, let's look at some specific critical thinking skills and see how they're used in business.

Before going on to the next chapter, here are some practice exercises for you to do.

Determine which statements are true.

1. Critical thinking is reserved for engineers, doctors and lawyers.

2. A critical thinker will listen to an opposing point of view.

3. People who think critically are judgmental, critical and negative.

4. A person who thinks critically also thinks comprehensively – they look at all the angles.

5. Critical thinking is a set of thinking skills that can be learned. However, some people seem to have some of these skills without formal training.

6. Many business decisions are made during lunch or on the golf course. This proves that critical thinking is reserved for use only at the board room and is used only by the top echelons of a company.

7. Factory workers are incapable of thinking critically because they lack "high order thinking skills"

8. The only difference between ordinary thinking and critical thinking is that critical thinking is used for urgent matters.

9. A clerk working at a supermarket observes that when a half case of bread is displayed, it sells more quickly because people think that the store will run out of it soon. This is an example of critical thinking.

10. A sales manager is opposed to training his sales force in critical thinking because he's worried they will use critical thinking to argue for a higher commissions. This is an example of critical thinking by the manager.

Now it's your turn. Create some statements about critical thinking that are true and create some that are false. Provide a brief explanation for each.

1. My statement:

My explanation:

2. My statement

My explanation:

Read various definitions of critical thinking.

http://lonestar.texas.net/~mseifert/crit2.html . Michael Scriven and Richard Paul "A Working Definition of Critical Thinking".

http://www.ncrel.org/sdrs/areas/issues/envrnmnt/drugfree/sa3crit.htm. Paul, Binker, Jensen, and Kreklau. "Critical Thinking Skills" 35 Dimensions of Critical Thinking

http://www.asa3.org/ASA/education/think/critical.htm#critical-thinking. Craig Rusbult "What is Critical Thinking? Critical Thinking in Education".

http://libguides.uhcl.edu/content.php?pid=191383&sid=1654549 University of Houston, Library Guides.

http://www.ius.edu/ilte/pdf/critical_thinking_handout_fall_02.pdf - Some Definitions of CT Source: IUS.edu

Having read several different definitions of critical thinking, which one do you like the best?

Create your own definition. If someone were to ask you, "what is critical thinking?" what would you say?

10

Assumptions–Can be Dangerous and Costly

Defining the Term

To assume means "to take for granted or to presuppose (Paul 1990 p541). The American Heritage Dictionary defines assumption as "a statement accepted or supposed true without proof of demonstration" (1985). Many of the decisions we make and actions we take are based upon assumptions. It's not always possible to have all the facts and know the truth. Paul states that "... people often equate making assumptions with making false assumptions." (Paul 1990, p541). He claims that when people say "Don't assume", they mean don't get trapped into making a false assumption. (Paul 1990).

Since "All human thought and experience are based on assumptions" (Paul and Elder 2001), it's impossible to avoid them. The issue is not with assumptions, but rather with "false assumptions" (Paul 1990). When we assume something and it turns out to be false – the result can be anything from an annoyance to a disaster. In certain professions, like engineering, it can be too dangerous to assume. Imagine an engineer assuming that a design for a bridge will work, but not testing out that design? Does that mean that every decision we make and every action we take must be tested and proven? In the business world and in many other professions, it isn't always possible to do this. Certain assumptions are quite reasonable. For example, it is reasonable to assume that people reading this book can understand English since it is written in English. It's also reasonable to assume, (though not a certainty) that people reading this book are interested in critical thinking. But other assumptions can be dangerous and costly.

Oftentimes, what a person thinks or believes "has not been consciously considered." (Lee 2002). Lee calls such assumptions "hidden assumptions" and states that an "important critical thinking skill is rooting out and challenging questionable assumptions." (Lee 2002) That, in fact is the basis of this chapter. As you'll discover, "a critical thinker understands that people have different assumptions ... [and] ... examines these assumptions." (Lee, 2002).

> People often equate making assumptions with making false assumptions.

Besides "hidden assumptions" (Paul 1990), Diestler distinguishes between "value assumptions" and "reality assumptions and states that value assumptions address the questions 'What is right'? and 'What should we do or be?" while "reality assumptions address the questions 'What is true and factual?' and 'What do we take for granted or as a given fact'?" (Diestler, 2001)

Value assumptions are beliefs about what is good and important that forms the basis of opinions on issues (Diestler p24). According to Diestler, there are many arguments that are based on "strongly held val-

12

ues that need to be understood (Diestler p24) and that issues that continue to be hotly contested often involve "cherished values on both sides" (Diestler p24). "These conflicting value assumptions can be between groups or individuals or within an individual (Diestler p25)

You can begin to see how such assumptions interfere with decisions and actions taking place within a business setting. Oftentimes a conflict can exist between groups or between individuals. Sometimes, as Diestler says, an individual can have a conflicting value assumption.

In a business setting, we are often concerned with both value and reality assumptions.

However, oftentimes we are concerned with "beliefs about what is true and factual about the world." (Diestler, p60).

"The fascinating element of assumptions is that they are often hidden to the people arguing for different conclusions." (Diestler p60). Critical thinkers examine "the reality assumptions of self and others that form the foundations of arguments." (Diestler p61). According to Diestler, "we need to examine the assumptions" (Diestler p62). However, we take a lot of things for granted. Some of what we believe simply isn't true. Do you believe that a heavier object will fall faster than a lighter object? If you were to drop a pencil and a dollar bill from the same height at the same time, which would hit the ground first? Back in the seventeenth century people believed the following: "The heavier something is, the faster it will fall."

Therefore, when two objects of different weight are dropped together, the heavier one will hit the ground before the lighter one. (Lee 2002)

I must admit that when I first read this it seemed to make sense and I thought that it might be true. Try it and see what happens. You'll discover that both objects hit the ground at the same time. (Note that in a classical experiment with feathers it was necessary to control air resistance by running the experiment in a vacuum.)

How many times have you made an assumption? How many times have you believed something to be true and based your argument on a false assumption?

Assuming the Experts are Right

You might be wondering what all this has to do with critical thinking in the work place and how assumptions are really dangerous and costly. How often have you relied upon the advice of an expert at your workplace? Usually, we assume that experts such as accountants, attorneys, management consultants, etc. are correct with their findings and their reports. These people are highly trained and are considered experts. But even experts can and do make mistakes and base their decisions on assumptions that are false.

Drucker claims that "many corporations are running on outdated business assumptions (Drucker p1 Theory of Business). He further states that companies that base their business theory on old outdated assumptions often "find themselves losing competitive ground and possibly failing or ending up in crisis (Drucker p1)

14

Critical thinkers seek evidence and facts. I'm not suggesting that you challenge your boss or supervisor on every decision. Nor am I suggesting that you automatically doubt the findings or reports from such experts as accountants, attorneys, etc. At the same time, I am not recommending that you automatically accept everything you read or hear as true, either. A certain amount of skepticism is healthy. In many work settings, there is a fine line between expressing general concern and challenging a superior. However, when workers rely on 'blind faith' and never challenge any assumption, that can be a prescription for disaster.

Scenario – Tardy Workers

Consider the following scenario where a medium size business had a problem with workers arriving late. The written Company policy stated that workers could be penalized for tardiness. The 'unofficial' policy was that workers should arrive five minutes before the start of the work day.

Despite several memos to employees about coming to work on time, workers continued to arrive late. Each employee was required to 'punch in' and have their time card stamped by a time clock. Management knew that employees were continuing to arrive late. So, they decided to get tough. They issued a memo stating that effective tomorrow, employees would lose a dollar for every minute that they were late! Management assumed that this action would solve the problem of employees coming late to work. The managers didn't bother to check with anyone to see how other businesses handled problems of this nature. They didn't look at the possible consequences of their actions. They just assumed the logistics would fall into place and they assumed that this would solve the problem. What happened next, really took management by surprise.

The next day nearly all the workers arrived about five minutes before the start of the work day. There were so many workers standing in line waiting to have their time card stamped by the clock that several workers were actually late for work by the time they had their time cards stamped. Management decided not to make any exceptions and 'docked' all the workers that were late. They continued with their policy and deducted one dollar from the salary of every worker who was late.

The workers complained bitterly and demanded to be paid. Other workers demanded to be paid for the extra 5-10 minutes they had to wait each morning in order to get their time card stamped on time. But management would not change the policy and assumed that the policy was working and that workers would adaptand accept the new arrangements.

After a few days, management was quite pleased that workers were finally reporting for work on time. But the work atmosphere was changing. Morale was low and an unofficial work slowdown began. Production began to slow down. A few workers quit and a few were fired.

By this time, the local papers had learned of the situation and started reporting it. Still, management stayed the course and would not change the policy. They assumed that they had a few disgruntled workers who would either quit or would be fired. But the situation continued to worsen. One of the workers called a local union representative and invited the union to come to the place of business and attempt to organize a union. The business was a non-union shop and the union happily accepted the invitation. But management wasn't happy at all and they decided to call the police and have the union representative removed from the premises. The police came and so did the press. The story made the headlines on all the local TV stations. Workers continued to quit and it became difficult to fill vacancies. The new policy proved disastrous. Management had based all their decisions on assumptions. Those assumptions proved to be wrong and very costly. Not all assumptions are this disastrous, but assumptions can be dangerous and costly.

Scenario #2 – The Sales Report

John was a sales manager in a large company. The Vice President of the company asked John to prepare a sales report and turn it in to the President on the following Monday. John decided to delegate the assignment to his star salesman named Bryan, who also served as a supervisor. John knew that Bryan was a very conscientious, hard working individual with a reputation for getting things done. When John gave Bryan the assignment, Bryan responded by saying, "You'll have it by Monday morning". John assumed that Bryan would complete the task on time.

However, a series of circumstances happened. Bryan received the assignment on Monday afternoon.

He had until the following Monday morning to get it done. He began clearing his schedule to work on the report and decided to finish whatever he could that day.

On Tuesday, Bryan's time and attention was diverted to a crisis within the Company. He had to put aside all his other work and deal with the crisis. On Wednesday, Bryan was still catching up on his regular work and hadn't even started the report. But he did manage to get caught up and cleared his schedule for Thursday. However, on Thursday, a nasty computer virus hit the Company's computer network and all computers were shut down by the IT department for most of the day. Bryan needed certain files that were on the system to complete the sales report.

---

linear thinking:
problems have only one solution and do not affect the rest of the organization and once a solution is found, it remains valid.

system thinking:
problems are complex, have more than one cause and more than one solution.

Finally, on Friday, Bryan began to work on the sales report. He spent most of the day working on the report and realized that he'd have to work throughout the weekend to get it done. He could come in on Saturdfay or work at home. Bryan decided he'd work throughout the entire weekend at home.

On Monday morning, John was checking his voicemail and received a call from Bryan's wife. She informed him that her husband had been taken to the hospital and was recovering from an emergency appendectomy during the weekend and could not finish the report! Within one hour, John had to go into the President's office and turn in the sales report. John was being considered for a promotion. Now he'd be lucky if he could keep his job!

The Need to Identify and Challenge Assumptions

In both of these scenarios, assumptions were made. In the first scenario, management made a false assumption and continued to enforce a poorly designed policy. Rather than using critical thinking and analyzing the situation, they used linear thinking, where "problems have only one solution and do not affect the rest of the organization and once a solution is found, it remains constantly valid (Montana and Charnov (pg 89) [Management, Barons Educational Series, Inc 2000] They just assumed that their action would correct the problem of tardy workers. This is contrary to system thinking which "asserts that problems are complex, have more than one cause and more than one solution (Montana and Charnov). This is actually a type of critical thinking.

In the second scenario, John assumed his top salesman would get the job done. In both scenarios, analysis and planning for alternatives were lacking. In both scenarios, the assumptions proved false and there were definite consequences. Both scenarios demonstrated a lack of planning, analysis and lack of a backup plan. In both scenarios, no one ever challenged the decision (assumption). No one ever even considered "what if ...?" No one challenged any assumption. Everything was taken for granted.

Chapter Summary

- Assumptions are statements that are taken for granted.
- Assumptions are statements that are supposedly true, but lack any proof.
- Many of the decisions we make are based upon assumptions.
- When people say "Don't Assume", what they really mean is don't base statements on false assumptions. False assumptions occur when you assume something is true, but later you discover that it is false.
- Assumptions can be classified as reality assumptions and value assumptions (Diestler 2001). Reality assumptions deal with issues about what is true, while value assumptions address issues about what is right.
- Critical thinkers identify assumptions and challenge them. "Assumptions should be examined in the light of the best information available ..." (Diestler p65). Assumptions can be challenged by asking such questions as "how do I know this is so?" or "what evidence is there to support this idea" or, expressed another way, "what makes you think or believe that?"
- Critical thinkers have a "curious and questioning attitude about reality and particularly about reality assumptions" (Diestler p69). They "look for solid evidence before accepting or advocating a viewpoint" (Diestler).

[Read the following scenario. Then identify the assumptions.]

The Move to the Suburbs

A repair shop that primarily fixes computers and other small electronic appliances has been in business for nearly 30 years in an urban location. The demographics of the city have changed and the younger population has moved out to the suburbs. The current location of the shop has very limited parking. In addition, because of traffic flow, it is difficult to get out of their tiny parking lot as traffic on that street has steadily increased over the years.

The Shop believes it is in their best interest to relocate to the suburbs—about a 20 minute drive over the highway—since the population of the city has become elderly and sales are down. The elderly population is very loyal to the Shop, but the number of sales are gradually dwindling. A number of Board Members who live in the suburban location have convince the majority of Board Members to purchase a parcel of land and build a new building.

Here is what a special committee reported to the Board.

They found a site approximately 3 acres about 20 minutes from the present location. The property has a stream that runs through the eastern side of the property. However, the Committee claims "wetland" is not a problem.

21

If approved, the Shop would purchase the land subject to an agreement with a neighboring vocational school. The plan calls for the school to purchase the land and wait until the Shop gets a subdivision.

The Zoning Board of the Town has expressed some concern about access onto an existing road that is behind the property. The Shop claims that if necessary, they would build their own private roadway and provide a huge parking lot for their customers. Their present location in the city has very limited parking.

Financial Considerations

Cost of property is $1.5 million. With the school, the Shop plans to offer $1 million. The minimum cost is $700,000 and maximum is $850,000.

Funding

The Shop plans to mortgage the current building for 6-7.5% interest. Their current assets were earning 10% last year and they believe they'll earn 10% next year as well.

The Shop believes:

1. The Zoning Board will approve the sale and construction of a building because it is a semi commercial zone and there isn't a repair shop in that section of the town.

2. Building time 1-2 years.

3. Building size is approximate 12,000 sq. ft. at approximately $225 a sq. ft.

4. The actual design for the building doesn't exist at this time.

5. The Shop believes that they'll have more business in the suburbs and that they will be able to charge more because the area is "upscale".

6. The Shop anticipates that they will be able to get apprentices from the vocational school who will work for free or at minimum wage.

Additional Information

1. If the plan fails there are no plans to fix up the current building or do anything to bring in new customers. Currently, there is no marketing plan for the new building.

2. It would cost approximately $150,000 to renovate the current building.

3. It is not known where the current population in the suburbs goes to get their computers and/or small appliances repaired.

4. The Board approved the motion to proceed with the purchase and the Chairman praised the Board for their excellent leadership. Not everyone is happy with the decision. Two board members resigned and one has stated that he will not seek another term and strongly disagrees with their decision.

What's wrong with this picture? Identify the assumptions and speculations. What would you recommend? List the assumptions you've identified and your recommendation

More Assumption Exercises

For each statement, identify whether it is an assumption or a fact and explain why.

Example: *The sales meeting is at 3 pm today. This is a fact and can be proven.*

Example: *The sales meeting will probably be long and boring. This is an assumption. It is unknown whether or not the meeting will be long and boring.*

1. Sales were good last month, so they should be even better this month.

2. We can easily capture 2% more of the market

3. Our accounting department has never made a mistake—as far as I know.

4. It's going to be a nice sunny day for our Company picnic.

5. There is no need to change our manufacturing procedures because they are working fine the way they are.

6. You get what you pay for.

7. Our department manager always starts the meeting on time.

8. Social media is a bunch of hype that doesn't work.

9. If we spend more on marketing, sales will go up.

10. We haven't done business with this company for years, because they did a terrible job back then. They're probably no different now.

11. Our factory workers aren't bright enough to suggest any ideas to us.

12. If I can get to work on time during a snow storm (and have an 8 mile drive), then everyone else should be able to get here on time.

13. All service technicians must wear an ID badge when making a service call.

14. The only way to assure workers come to work on time is to use a time clock.

15. Dave has been late 3 times this week. He'll probably be late today.

16. The last training session we had was a waste of time. This one will be no different.

17. If you work hard, you will get a promotion.

18. If a file was saved on the computer, it is there somewhere, unless it was deleted.

19. We have a copyright on our materials and a watermark as well. No one is going to steal our materials.

20. If an employee is caught stealing from the Company, that person will be fired.

21. The Company always has a holiday party in December.

22. No one can make a better product than we make.

23. We had 12 people apply for the sales manager position.

24. Jack has worked for this Company for 20 years.

25. No one working for this Company would post a negative comment on our social media site.

26. Sales usually go down during the summer so this season shouldn't be any different.

27. One is either a responsible employee or not. There's no excuse for being late.

28. This training program will be like the last one—a waste of time.

29. You need to understand and know your product in order to sell it successfully.

30. Everyone has a need for our product.

31. I'm in a hurry to make some copies. The copier will probably jam.

More About Assumptions

Identify an assumption you make recently at work:

Have you ever done the following: Decided to use a particular vendor because you had a good experience and assumed that the quality of service would remain the same?

Identify a time you made a decision based upon an assumption. Did the assumption prove to be true or false?

Looking back over a recent day at work, list several assumptions that you made and note which ones proved to be false:

Pick one assumption that you listed above. How could you have determined whether or not your assumption was true or false? Was there any way that you could have determined this – by asking questions, doing a test, seeking information from someone, etc?

Identify a time you made a decision based upon an assumption. Did the assumption prove to be true or false?

Looking back over a recent day at work, list several assumptions that you made and note which ones proved to be false:

Pick one assumption that you listed above. How could you have determined whether or not your assumption was true or false? Was there any way that you could have determined this – by asking questions, doing a test, seeking information from someone, etc?

Asking Critical Thinking Questions

Questioning can be used to clarify, seek evidence, challenge assumptions and challenge biased and flawed thinking. Years ago, when I had my first sales job, my supervisor told me that if customers are asking questions, they're buying. Most salespeople recognize the importance of questions, both from the customer's perspective and from the salesperson's perspective as well.

But questioning and more specifically, asking critical thinking questions is not limited to salespeople. One of the mainstreams of critical thinking is seeking evidence or proof that something is true. Critical Thinking is based on Socratic Questioning (which will be discussed later).

To make a good decision, one needs some information and questioning is a great way to get that information. There are a number of critical thinking questions that are designed to seek evidence. Richard Paul (1990) presents a number of questions to ask that " ...probe reasons and evidence" (p276). The following questions have been adapted from his material:

- Can you give me an example?
- How do you know that?

31

- What makes you think that is true?
- Do you have any evidence or proof?
- What makes you say that?
- Can you explain why you believe that?
- Is there any reason to doubt that evidence?
- How do we know this is true? How can we find out?

Asking these types of questions actually requires the speaker to think critically and provide you with some reasons. If they can't provide you with any reasons, then there's not much of an argument. At that point what they're saying is merely their opinion. But if they can back it up with facts, then they may have a valid argument. However, there is a caveat here. The answers you get may require further probing and clarification.

If you need further clarification, Paul recommends the following questions which I have adapted from his material (p276).

- What do you mean when you say … ?
- What's your main point?
- Could you explain that another way?
- Are you saying _____ or _____?
- Can you give me an example?
- Why do you think that is so?

Recall in an earlier chapter on Assumptions, that assumptions need to be challenged. To help you do that, Paul (276) recommends the following questions which I have also adapted:

- Is that an assumption or a fact?
- What are you assuming?
- How do you know that to be true?
- Is this always true?

In all of these examples, these are not the only questions that you could ask. They are only meant to serve as some examples.

Questioning can also be used regarding viewpoints or perspectives. In a future chapter I will talk about frames of reference. Here are some issues that specifically address questions regarding a person's frame of reference or perspective:

- How might other groups of people respond? What would influence them?
- What might someone from a different perspective think?
- What might someone who disagrees say?
- Why have you chosen this particular perspective?

(Adapted from Paul (p276).

There are also questions that probe implications and consequences. Paul (1990) suggests these types of questions:

- What are you implying?
- If that were to happen, what else might happen?
- What would be the result?

- What that necessarily happen or probably happen?
- Is there an alternative?

Finally, there are even questions to ask about questions:

- How can we determine this?
- Does this question assume anything?
- How would someone else answer this question?
- Do we really understand the question? What is being asked?
- Why is this question important?

(Adapted from Paul 1990).

As you can see that are all sorts of questions that can be asked. The use of questioning can be very effective in getting information and clarifying it. However, the use of questions can also help someone to think critically. When you ask a question like, "do you have any evidence to support that idea?" you are requiring the person to think critically.

I'd like to offer you some suggestions about using questions. Be careful with "why" questions. They tend to put people on the defensive and can be designed solely to manipulate someone. Example: "Why did you do that?" Oftentimes when someone asks a question like this, they really don't want to know why you did that. Rather, they're indirectly saying, I didn't like what you did. This is not critical thinking.

> "Why" questions put people on the defensive. Often, they are implied criticism.

There are times when a "why" question is justified. However, a better way of asking a why question is, "can you give me a reason?" or "what made you decide to take this action?" Distress impairs thinking (which will be discussed later) and makes critical thinking all but impossible. So, choose your questions carefully.

Oftentimes in my training sessions, someone will say, "this may be a dumb question, but ..." and then ask me a question. I always respond initially, that there are no dumb questions. Chances are if you have a question, someone else in the room has the same question as well. However, there is a difference between an ordinary question and a question that requires critical thinking. A critical thinking question will either seek evidence, challenge an assumption, clarify or challenge a flawed statement.

Challenging flawed thinking is much like challenging an assumption or seeking evidence. Here's an example of flawed thinking:

In discussing what caterer to choose for a corporate event the program planner says, I once went to an event catered by the XYZ Caterers and it was horrible. Another person says, but they're one of the largest catering companies. What was the problem? (clarifying question).

The dialogue continues:

Planner – the food was terrible. The hot dishes were cold and the food didn't taste good at all.

Committee member – How do you explain the fact that this company has been in business for years? They're the largest catering company in the area!

Planner – I don't know, but I'm telling you the food was awful.

Committee Member – How can we get more information about this Caterer?

Planner – you can call them if you want, but I'm sure they're not going to tell you why they screwed up (assumption). I'd never use them if it were up to me. (a categorical statement – absolute word "never").

In this scenario, the planner is not answering the questions. All he's doing is saying don't use this Caterer's services. He's made a number of flawed statements. Here are some specific critical thinking questions to ask:

- Does one bad event mean that every event the caterer does will be bad?
- What were the reasons why this meal was bad?
- Has anyone else had a bad experience with this company?
- How can we find out what happened?

You can see how flawed thinking by just one person can influence others. You can also see how critical thinking questions can help clarify a situation.

36

There's a book called <u>Asking the Right Questions: A Guide to Critical Thinking</u>, (Sixth Edition. by M. Neil Browne and Stuart Keeley. Prentice Hall Copyright: 2001.) that you may wish to read. It's important to ask questions, especially the right questions.

Summary

Questioning is an effective way to get information

Critical thinking questions clarify, seek evidence, challenge assumptions and challenge biased and flawed thinking

Questioning can also be used to help people to think critically, by asking them to provide some type of evidence for their statement or belief.

An effective way to challenge an assumption is to ask a question that seeks evidence

Exercise: Asking Questions

I once went to an event catered by the XYZ Caterers and it was horrible.

What questions can you ask here that would be appropriate? (Hint – assumption).

The food was terrible. The hot dishes were cold and the food didn't taste good at all. What questions could you ask in response to this statement?

I'd never use them if it were up to me. What's the problem with this statement? What would be an appropriate question to ask?

Scenario

A business hired a contractor to replace a flue pipe that runs from the furnace to the roof and vents exhaust. The contractor replaced that pipe and in addition replace a flue pipe on a hot water heater. According to the Gas Company, there was nothing wrong with the flue pipe on the hot water heater.

The Business then called the State Business Regulations for Contractors Department and inquired if a written contract was required as none was ever given. A person who answered the call replied that yes, a contact was indeed required before the Contractor could proceed. However when Business called to the same Department again to follow-up, a different person answered the phone and reported that no written contract was necessary in order to have the work done. The Business refused to pay for the replacement of the hot water heater flue and the contractor disputed the lack of payment.

What questions would you ask the Contractor?

What questions would you ask the State?

What questions would you ask the Gas Company?

Can you see how asking questions would help you resolve this problem or at least get you valuable information?

Asking Questions

Create a list of questions to ask regarding knowledge.

1.

2.

3.

4.

5.

Ask questions that demonstrate comprehension

1.

2.

3.

4.

Ask questions that pertain to application - such as using knowledge and facts to solve problems.

1.

2.

3.

4.

Ask questions pertaining to analysis (making inferences and seeking evidence.

1.

2.

3.

4.

Ask questions that pertain to evaluating.

1.

2.

3.

4.

5.

Ask questions that pertain to creation/synthesis (gathering information in different ways

1.

2.

3.

For further information go to
http://www.ucdoer.ie/index.php/How_to_Ask_Questions_that_Prompt_Critic al_Thinking University College Dublin

The following questions have been adapted from Richard Paul **(p.276)**

Critical Thinking Questions:
- Probe for Reason and Evidence
- Clarify
- Challenge Assumptions
- Identify Frames of Reference
- Focus on Implications or Consequences
- Question about questions

Questions that Probe for Reason and Evidence

- Can you give me an example?
- How do you know that?
- What makes you think that is true?
- Do you have any evidence or proof?

For each of the exercises that follow, ask some questions about a specific situation you are experiencing.

Ask some questions that prove for reason and evidence:

1.

2.

3.

Clarifying Questions

- What do you mean when you say … ?
- What's your main point?
- Could you explain that another way?

Ask some questions that clarify:

1.

2.

Questions about Assumptions

- Is that an assumption or a fact?
- What are you assuming?
- How do you know that to be true?

Ask some questions about assumptions

1.

2.

3.

Questions about Frames of Reference

- What might someone with a different perspective think?
- What might someone who disagrees say?
- How might other groups of people respond? What would influence them?

Ask some questions about Frames of References:

1.

2.

3.

More Questions

Questions about implications

- What are you implying?
- If that were to happen, what else might happen?

Ask some questions about implications:

1.

2.

Questions about Questions

- How can we determine this?
- Does this question assume anything?

Ask some questions regarding questions:

1.

2.

Frames of Reference

What is a frame of reference? A frame of reference is a critical thinking skill that means point of view or perspective. Swartz defines it as "a person's most basic beliefs and values" (Swartz 1990, p112). A frame of reference "is shaped by our prior knowledge, assumptions, values, or language, about others" (Teays p27). Assumptions (as discussed in Chapter 2) and values can influence our perceptions (Teays p27). How frames of reference impact upon the business world is the main focus of this chapter.

According to Teays, "[t]he frame of reference influences the ways issues are presented and potentially "stacks the deck" for one interpretation versus another (Teays p30). This becomes quite important in negotiation and it certainly helps to understand an adversary's point of view. Wolff claims that "differing assumptions and value systems ... give rise to conflicting testimony and interpretations" (Wolff 1986, 37) "Each of us has a particular vantage point from which events are seen and understood" Bradford (1994) identifies that individual frames of reference interfere with business meetings as will be discussed later in this chapter.

"Our knowledge grows when we recognize diverse perspectives ... "(Teays, p31). Sometimes in the business world, frames of reference are simply called frames. Pinkley and Northcraft (Feb 1994 v37 n1 p193(13) have "explored the influence of cognitive frames on negotiation processes and outcomes". They have found that "... frames significantly influence the processes and outcomes of conflict .... By frames, they are talking about perspectives that people have. Pinkley states it best when he says, "Conflict frames are the lenses through which disputants view a conflict situation" (Pinkley, 1990). and "conflict frames determine what issues disputants believe need to be negotiated and specified in a settlement" (Pinkley and Northcraft)

People "frame or experience" a conflict in different ways (Pinkley and Northcraft), thus making it difficult to resolve. People in a conflict have different frames of reference and subjective experiences that are their reality and thus determines the nature of the conflict for them." (Klar, Bar-Tal, & Kruglanski, 1987, p193).

In terms of resolving conflicts, Pinkley and Northcraft state, "it may be important to determine if managers can learn to recognize the conflict frames of others and whether such information is of strategic use in negotiations." Thus, it appears that the business world could benefit by understanding conflict frames as stated by Pinkly and Northcraft:

Conflict frames may provide an important tool both for improving the quality of negotiated agreements and for enhancing the ability to resolve disputes among organization members. (Pinkley and Northcraft)

46

Recognizing a frame of reference would not only be helpful in resolving conflicts but would also help to improve meetings. According to Bradford (1994), a manager told him that in most of the meetings she attended "95 % of the time is caught up in jockeying for power and other such activities unrelated to the purpose of the meeting" (Bradford, 1994).

The ability to recognize frames of reference goes beyond resolving conflicts and business meetings. Think of how many interactions in the office, business deals and sales could be better facilitated if managers and other workers could recognize frames of reference. Sometimes they are easy to recognize and other times they are much more subtle. While there may be subtle clues to one's frame of reference – the actual frame of reference of an individual can be quite strong and persistent.

Consider a customer who has had a bad experience with a particular business. That customer is unlikely to buy from that company again. But, frames of reference can be much more subtle and indirectly influence an individual's thinking and decision making.

Take the case of an office manager who had a bad experience with chemicals, particularly office cleaning chemicals. She had a sensitivity to certain cleaning solutions and actually became ill from the odor. Now this same manager is in a position to decide whether or not to buy a new copier for the office. The new copier is set up in a small and poorly ventilated room. She detects an odor coming from the copier. Immediately, her frame of reference is one of noxious chemicals and her sensitivity to them. She decides not to buy this particular copying machine. Her frame of reference greatly influences her decision not to buy.

Our frames of reference influence our thinking and our decision making. Not only do we need to identify our own frames of reference, but we need to be able to identify other people's frames of reference as well. With any book or magazine, there are at least two frames of reference – the author's and the reader's. If there are characters in the book or magazine, they may have a frame of reference different from your own or the author's perspective. Since each person has his own frame of reference, you can begin to imagine the difficulty of reaching an agreement at a business meeting where everyone has their own personal perspective. As was stated earlier by Bradford, oftentimes an individual's frame of reference concerns "jockeying for power" (Bradford), rather than the actual topic for discussion. "Conflict frames …" Pinkley and Northcraft) provide an even greater challenge.

The first step in understanding someone's frame of reference is to recognize that we all have our own frames of reference. In heated arguments it becomes easy to recognize frames of reference. Opponents oftentimes become polarized. The situation is sometimes exacerbated when people sit at opposite sides of a table so that they physically oppose each other as well.

The importance of being able to identify a frame of reference cannot be underestimated. Wolff, (Educational Leadership October 1986), claims that even a researcher's "use of evidence will be influenced by his or her frame of reference" (p38). Wolff has developed a frame of reference model that is "based on a conception of the relationship between an author's frame of reference and what he or she writes" (Wolff 1986, p37). The model consists of two different descriptions of the "relationships between the !Kung men and women" (Wolff 1986, p39). When the two accounts are compared and contrasted, the results are astounding. Initially, no one can believe that the descriptions are actually of the same culture of people.

Recognizing a Frame of Reference

When I taught Critical Thinking at the undergraduate level, there was an exercise I gave to my students. It was actually a real problem. A man's face was turning purple. He went to his doctor who examined him and did all sorts of tests. All of the tests came back negative and his doctor could offer no medical explanation of why this man's face was turning purple.

It was interesting to me to see the various frames of reference the students used. One particular class consisted of nursing students. They offered all sorts of medical reasons why this man's face was turning purple. In my other classes, consisting of a general across the board mixture of majors, I received a variety of responses that reflected various frames of reference.

This particular exercise was actually designed to demonstrate cause and effect. But it was interesting to me to see the various frames of reference being displayed. By the way, there was no medical explanation for this man's face turning purple. What caused it? He had received a set of purple towels for Christmas and didn't heed the warning to wash the towels before using. Every time he dried his face, the purple dye was transferred to his face. It was only after he changed towels that he realized what had happened. The doctors didn't recognize this because their frame of reference was medical. They never considered any other cause.

This story demonstrates the importance of frames of reference and how a particular frame can actually limit our thinking and our options. When it comes to making decisions and solving problems, it's important to recognize that we all have frames of reference and that they can greatly influence our thinking and decision making. A good question to ask yourself to help you identify your own frame of reference is: why am I thinking like this? This is an excellent question to ask yourself when you are attempting to solve a problem or make a decision. When you do this you are, in essence, thinking about your thinking, which is actually another critical skill called metacognition, which will be discussed in another chapter.

Frames of Reference as a Reflection of Bias.

Another way of viewing a frame of reference is to realize that everyone has their own bias and that frames of reference reflect such bias. Wolff states that there is a danger that students will "come to accept more premises uncritically as common knowledge" (Wolff 1986, p37) unless they recognize that information presented to them "was developed by people with ..." (p37) biases of their own. Whether we hear or read something, we need to think critically and attempt to identify the author's or speaker's frame of reference. We may agree or disagree with what we hear or read. But it is helpful to recognize where the speaker or author is coming from – meaning what is his/her frame of reference.

Sometimes, in a controversial matter, both sides overstate their position, despite their good intentions. In other matters where there really isn't any controversy, you might think that there is no big deal, that the outcome doesn't matter that much. It may not matter to one person, but it may be of great importance to someone else – depending upon his/her frame of reference. Oftentimes at a business meeting, what initially appears to be unimportant results in a lengthy discussion. It may be unimportant to some people, but to others, it's quite important. In matters like this, it is very unwise to assume. (See chapter on Assumptions).

Our biases are reflected in our frames of reference. Bias in this sense is not necessarily a bad ideology, but rather it is a reflection of our preference or particular mode of thinking. People's frames of reference usually become clearer as they speak and respond to us.

Wolff however emphasizes stressing the "values and difficulty of arriving at a consensus about reality, rather than to unmask the biases of various authors" (Wolff 1986)

Two different accounts of the same topic.

Consider these two different descriptions of the same company.

   Description #1 – A small company has clearly demonstrated that the American Dream is alive and well. What began as a small store emphasizing bargain prices for consumers has become one of the most successful retail chains in the world. This highly successful company has done more to employ people and keep prices low so consumers can still get a bargain. The giant retailer has set a precedent and changed the way retail companies do business. For years it was the manufacturer that dictated the price. Whenever the manufacturer raised their price, retailers were forced into raising their retail price as well. The result being the consumer paid more. But this highly successful company buys in such high volume that they actually tell the manufacturer what they will pay and if the wholesale price is too high, the manufacturer must lower it or lose business. In some instances when the manufacturer refused to lower their prices, the Company refused to buy any more of their products, thus putting tremendous pressure on them to lower their prices or lose a substantial amount of sales! Never before has a retail company ever been able to do this – to dictate to manufacturers what they will pay for their goods. Thus, they are able to continuously provide bargains for the consumers.

The great things that this Company has done are not limited to the US. The Company has gone to foreign markets to buy goods at lower costs. This has resulted in thousands of people in poor countries who were unemployed, now being employed. These same people who had no work at all are now drawing a paycheck each week. In addition, the Company insists on high quality and good working conditions and they actually inspect foreign factories. Americans should take pride in the great accomplishments of this Company.

Description #2 A company which began as a small business has grown to gigantic proportions and in the process has put hundreds of small neighborhood businesses out of business and cost thousands of people their jobs. But the damage didn't stop there. This Company buys in such high volume that they actually dictate the price of wholesale goods. If a manufacturer refuses to lower their price, the Company ceases to do business with that manufacturer. In many instances, the manufacturer simply couldn't afford to lower their prices. Their cost of operation and cost of raw materials had increased. However, once the Company stopped doing business with the manufacturer, sales plummeted so low that the manufacturer was forced to go out of business. Thousands of people lost their jobs.

They were eventually forced to go to work at the very business that put them out of work, of course at considerable lower wages, or remain unemployed.

One might be able to rationalize that at least the Company continues to offer bargains to consumers. However, this really isn't the case. To be sure, there are some bargains this Company offers. But those are the lead items at the front of each store. As one goes down the aisle one discovers, (if paying attention) that the other items are considerably higher, even higher than competitor retail stores! But many people are fooled when they see the initially low priced items as they enter the store and end up actually paying more than what the same product would cost in another retail store!

The Company has faced and lost a class action suit by workers for unfair working conditions. But what goes on in this country is nothing compared to what happens overseas. The Company does business in several foreign countries. They have created factories which are staffed by "slave laborers" earning $.17 an hour or less! These workers are forced to work very long hours with no overtime. Even in a foreign country where the cost of living is considerably less than the US, $.17 an hour or less can only be described as "slave labor". There have been documented stories on TV about this. The Company is exploiting foreign workers, yet claiming they are helping

54

the economies of these foreign countries. Americans should be ashamed of what this Company is doing. (In case you haven't identified the Company yet – it is WalMart)

Strategies for Identifying Frames of Reference:

Beyer has developed a series of steps to identify what he calls "a point of view" (Beyer 1988, p342). He emphasized identifying "the subject or topic being presented" (p342) and the "words or phrases that suggest how the author personally feels about the subject" (p342). In the next step, Beyer (1988) recommends identifying "any unstated assumptions" (p342). He also recommends looking for aspects of the subject that have not been mentioned. The last two steps include identifying the author's position (Beyer 1988, p342) and stating "what the author must believe" (p342).

Summary

- A frame of reference is a perspective or point of view.
- Frames of reference influence the way issues are presented.
- Frames of reference significantly influence the processes and outcomes of conflict (Pinkley and Northcraft)
- The business world could benefit by understanding conflict frames.
- Business meetings, conflicts and decisions can be greatly affected by various frames of reference.

- It is important to identify and recognize your own frame of reference.

Frames of Reference

A Frame of Reference is a viewpoint or perspective. Identify the frame of reference for each of the following positions:

- An accountant
- A marketing person
- A Sales person
- A Lawyer
- A CEO
- A Sales Manager
- A job applicant
- A doctor
- A fireman
- A racist

In each scenario, identify the likely frame of reference:

A convenience store wants to build a store in a residential area. What is their likely frame of reference? (There may be several of them).

A group of IT specialists are attending a presentation on a new software package. What might be their frame of reference? What might be the presenter's frame of reference?

The accounting department is going to be audited by the IRS. What is the likely frame of reference of the accountants?

The Sales Department has just been given a new quota. What might be their perspective about this? (There may be more than one perspective).

A worker was injured on the job. What might be the worker's perspective and what might be the employer's perspective?

A customer is having difficulty with a computer accessory not working. He spoke to tech support, but didn't get the problem resolved. Now he is chatting online with live tech support and his text has an angry tone. What might be his frame of reference? What might be the customer service rep's frame of reference.

For each of the following, identify what business you would choose and why. As you identify "why" you are actually relating to your frame of reference.

Where would you buy a Pizza

Bouquet of flowers

Television

What company would you choose to buy a

Computer

A Printer

A Microwave Oven

A Digital Camera

To hire a caterer

Where would you buy a new winter coat?

Where would you buy automotive supplies

Where would you buy sundries (toothbrushes, hairbrush, shampoo, etc)

Would you buy any particular brand. If yes, why?

Identify your own personal frame of reference for each situation. First, identify your thought. Then identify your frame of reference.

You always buy a loaf of bread each week. Today you notice that it costs 10 cents more.

You are called in to meet with your supervisor for your annual review.

You arrive at work and a co-worker tells you – "The boss wants to see you, right now!"

On your way to work, you get stuck in an unexpected traffic jam.

You and your entire department receive an award and special commendation for doing such a great job on a project you just completed.

You learn that several people have gotten "pink slips" today.

You meet a newly hired employee.

You turn on your computer and can't find the file you need.

A group of workers invite you to join them for lunch at a local pizza shop. You've eaten there before and didn't like it.

You've been assigned to work on a Project and you don't understand how to work on it.

You've just been informed that your current Supervisor is leaving and you will getting a new supervisor beginning next week.

Your Christmas bonus is less than what you received last year and even less than what new employees have received.

You meet another employee in the central supply room and noticed that she didn't list all the supplies she took with her.

You have a special pen that you like to use. It was on your desk when you left for lunch and now you can't find it.

The Company informs you that next week there will be a half day training program.

More Frames of Reference

In the following scenarios, please identify each person's frame of reference

1. Your Company is meeting and negotiating with a group of neighbors. Your Company want to build a fast food restaurant in their neighborhood The group consists of three neighbors. One is an older woman who has been living in the neighborhood for all her life. The other is a younger woman who has only lived there for two years. The third person is the President of the Neighborhood Council and is an experienced negotiator. Identify each person's probable frame of reference. Also, identify your frame of reference as you do this exercise.

2. Your neighbor has invited you and several other people for an outdoor barbeque. Identify each person's frame of reference:

- A fireman
- A young man who has just worked out at gym
- A vegetarian
- What is your own frame of reference?

3. Your Company is hiring a new CEO and you have been invited to serve on the hiring committee. You don't know the other people servicing on the committee, but you do know their name and title. Identify each person's frame of reference:

- The senior VP of the Company
- An accountant
- Human Resources
- A marketing representative
- A retired consultant who has been with the Company for years

4. You have called a meeting of your Department because your department has failed to complete a Project on time. Identify each employee's frame of reference.

- Mary—a conscientious worker who often misunderstands or gets confused about instructions.
- Paul—a team player who is big on collaboration
- Jay—prefers to work on tasks alone

Are you making any assumptions?

5. You supervise two other employees and have been asked by your boss to work on a special project. Identify each employee's frame of reference

- Nelson a veteran of the Gulf War who runs a "tight ship"
- Gladys – who is very creative, very much right brain oriented

6. Your Company is about to launch a major Social Media campaign to market your products.

- Larry is very negative about the campaign— What is his likely frame of reference
- Sharon—prides herself as being a "positive thinker" What is her likely frame of reference.

7. You interview a candidate for a position and the candidate is poorly dressed, chewing gum, arrived late, is argumentative, aggressive and demands to know about salary and benefits. (The position is not a sales position).

- What is this candidate's frame of reference?
- What is your frame of reference?

How to discover someone's frame of reference.

An easy way to learn about someone's frame of reference is simply to ask them why they think what they are thinking.

Scenario—A colleague of yours tells you that he thinks the Company is going to lay people off after Christmas. You ask him why he thinks that and he tells you, "I worked for another Company. After Christmas they laid off a lot of people".

If you want to probe for an assumption ask this person what evidence does he have other than what he's just stated. If this person is making an assumption, there will be little if any evidence to support the assumption.

Now it's your turn:

Create a little scenario, which can be real or imaginary. Identify a question to ask that would identify a frame of reference. (Usually asking "what makes you think that" will suffice). If their response appears to be an assumption – probe for an assumptions by asking "What evidence do you have to support what you are saying?"

65

Frames of Reference— Part Two

Perception of Buyer's Price and Value

The previous section dealt with Frames of Reference in general and some specific application to the business/work environment. This section will be of particular interest to managers, sales people and marketers as it will deal with how frames of reference affect a consumer's buying decision. According to Smith and Nagle (California Management Review, Fall p98), frames of reference can "change the relationship between what customers perceive they pay and what they perceive they get in return" (Nagle and Smith 1995). They define value in very simple terms, "what the customer gets in relation to what the customer gives" (Nagle and Smith p98).

Smith and Nagle (1995) claim that buyers often form frames of reference when making purchase decisions and that these frames of reference influence how buyers respond to pricing and product information. This is called "framing" (Smith & Nagle p98) and it is grounded in "prospect theory" (Smith & Nagle p98). Prospect theory combines the psychology of decision evaluations with the economic theory of consumer choice (Smith & Nagle p98). This theory claims that people evaluate purchases in terms of gains or losses, relative to a reference point (1995).

67

Based upon this theory, managers can influence the decisions buyers make by how they represent or "frame" price and benefits in relation to a reference point. (p100).

Here is how this works. A purchase decision by a consumer can be influenced depending upon how the information to the consumer is presented – whether is it presented as a gain or a loss. In their article Smith and Nagle present an example of two gas stations. The first one is selling gas for $1.30 a gallon (don't you wish it were so now!) and gives a $.10 discount if you pay with cash. The other gas station sells gas for $1.20 and charges a $.10 surcharge for using a credit card.

Which one offers the better deal? Which one would you choose? Economically speaking, the cost is the same at both gas stations. Yet, most people prefer to buy gas from the first station. The reason is "the perceived cost of purchasing" (Smith & Nagle, p100) from the first station is less than purchasing from the 2nd station, because the first one offers a discount, while the second station has a surcharge. According to prospect theory, "buyers judge a loss as more painful than they judge the gain of an equal amount as pleasurable" (p100). The second gas station actually discourages buyers from making purchases because it established a lower regular price of $1.20 as a reference point and in effect, "penalized" buyers who used a credit card with a perceived loss (p100).

The way a price is framed can influence a consumer. Most consumers have a reference point (frame of reference) regarding the cost of an item or service. A loss or even a perceived loss is painful to them.

"Managers can actually suggest frames of reference by designing transactions that reflect a gain and avoid a perceived loss." (Smith & Nagle p100). This knowledge is fascinating information and quite useful. Managers who study frames of reference and/or prospect theory know about it and know how to use it.

In addition to designing the transaction to reflect a gain and avoid a perceived loss, managers can also frame or describe the decision to buy as a gain or a loss and they can combine gains or losses as "bundles that increase the perceived value of the combination" (Smith and Nagle p100).

One of the ways a sale can be designed to reflect a gain and avoid a loss is by stating a higher price, then offering a discount. This is a familiar technique and you undoubtedly have experienced it. We routinely see items in circulars in newspapers and on TV as "on sale" with a discounted price. Once a frame of reference has been established, a discount is seen as a gain – you're getting more for your money.

Another way managers can influence consumers to purchase something is through a technique called "endowing" (Smith & Nagle p101). The technique involves giving the customer a trial product before the purchase. The theory behind this is that "it is more painful for consumers to give up an asset than it is pleasurable to obtain it" (Smith & Nagle p101). Thus, once a customer has an item, they are "biased in favor of retaining the status quo, of keeping the assets that they already 'own'" (Smith & Nagle p101). Some of this information may not be new to you. But what is probably new to you is that all of these techniques are based upon a customer's frame of reference. The theory goes as follows: "If buyers can be persuaded to take the product home, they will adjust their reference point to include the newly acquired asset" (Smith & Nagle p101). Thus, "buy now, pay later" is a frequent tactic used by many businesses.

Positive vs. Negative Framing of Purchase

Sometimes, for certain types of products and services, it is more effective to frame advertising in terms of the potential loss the consumers may associate with not buying the item or service. Such products as insurance, home security, pain relievers, mouthwash, etc, are often marketed with a negative frame of reference. (Smith & Nagle. p103). There is often pain associated if one lacks these products. For other products, it depends upon the product category. If you're a marketer, you probably know and are familiar with these techniques. However, I repeat again, that what may be new to you is that all these techniques are based upon a customer's frame of reference.

Bundling

In the computer business, various packages of software a "bundled" or put together and come with a new computer. However, there is another use of bundling. Sometimes managers "bundle" losses together. Smith and Nagle (1995) give an example of buying a new car stereo at the time of purchasing a new car. An additional $250 for a car stereo doesn't seem as much of an expense (loss) compared to a $20,000 car. The theory behind this is that "several separate losses are perceived as more painful than one large bundled loss" (Smith and Nagle p103). Thus, bundling losses together has a smaller effect than having separate losses.

Unbundling

Bundling can also be used for gains as well. When it's done for gains, it's actually called unbundling. The result is that the consumer perceives a gain, rather than loss. Nagle and Smith talk about magazine subscriptions that give new subscribers not just a magazine, but also a free bonus gift. According to Smith and Nagle, "Buyers perceive their utility to be more positively affected if multiple gains are offered separately, because several smaller gains are perceived as having more value than one large bundled gain" (Smith & Nagle, p103).

However, Smith and Nagle do state the following: "Anyone who thinks only in terms of objective economic values will find these principles farfetched" (p104). Buyers don't all act the same and prospect theory recognizes that. Smith and Nagle make that point and state, "There are different ways to frame the same transactions and each way implies somewhat different behavior" (Smith & Nagle, p104). Managers who are aware of this can change the way items are framed for sale, thus reducing the "... pain of higher prices ..." (Smith & Nagle, p104).

Framing the Formation of the Reference Price

For most consumers, a reference price (frame of reference for a price), is a major part of making a decision to purchase something. Businesses "frequently attempt to influence a customer's frame of reference by suggesting a new reference price." (Smith and

Nagle, p104). This is why many companies have a higher initial list price. When a consumer recalls the initial price and then sees the current price the customer's frame of reference has been established with a higher price. Oftentimes businesses offer a higher priced item at the top of a line which influences a buyer's reference price – since the remaining items in the line seem to be less expensive (Smith and Nagle). Studies have shown that "Adding a premium product to the product line... may enhance buyers' perceptions of lower-priced products in the product line ..." and may influence "Low-end buyers to trade up to higher-priced models." (Smith & Nagle p107). The "...addition of new premium products raises buyer's reference prices, making mid-price positions more acceptable." (Smith & Nagle p107)

Once again, I emphasize that all of this is based upon frames of reference. However, frames of reference concerning a price can also be influenced. The last price a customer pays has an especially strong influence on the reference price, "...because it's more likely to be recalled as a frame of reference than past prices that were observed but not paid" (Smith & Nagle p108). Another interesting point that the authors make is that "... numerous small price increases for frequently purchased items are more likely to be accepted than are infrequent large increases ..."Smith & Nagle p107). The reason for this is that buyers remember the last purchase price and will raise their reference price accordingly before they encounter the next increase. For that reason, the opposite is true regarding infrequently purchased items. The price of a car may not have increases any more than the cost of food over a 4 year time period, but since it's been four years since a consumer bought car, they are using an outdated frame of reference. (Smith & Nagle 1995). When they see the price of new car with four years of inflation added, the result is what car sales-people call "sticker shock".

Buyer's Perception of Price and Value

Weber-Fechner Law

The Weber-Fechner Law claims that people perceive the difference in price between two items proportionally rather than in absolute terms (Smith & Nagle). Smith and Nagle provide an example of a typewriter selling for $1000 and another one selling for $600. Everything else being equal, most people would choose the one selling for $600. In a second scenario, a word processor sells for $20,000 and another one of equal value sells for $19,600. The absolute value between both examples is $400. Yet, buyers in the second example perceive the price difference as only 2%. But the absolute difference in both scenarios is $400.

Another aspect of the Weber-Fechner Law is that people frame price differences relative to the purchase price, rather than calculate the exact difference. Smith and Nagle state that "...the perception of a price change depends on the percentage..." not the absolute difference..." (Smith and Nagle p111). This also implies that buyers will tolerate a series of small price increases better than one large increase. For example, at the time of this writing, gas prices are continuing to rise a few cents every few days. People really aren't complaining much. However if suddenly the price of gas went up say $5.00 or more in one day, motorists would be screaming mad and would probably start complaining, vigorously.

Summary

"In addition to framing, there are several ways that managers can influence buyer's perceptions of benefits and value by manipulating how the certainties of decision outcomes are expressed" (Smith and Nagle p113). Business researchers have discovered that "framing and the use of frames of reference" can be used "... to influence [consumers'] perceptions of price and value." Smith and Nagle state that "... there is a need to practice to understand how and why buyers respond to different ways of framing price, benefits and value (p114). The use of framing in a business setting is ... grounded in 'prospect theory'... "(Smith and Nagle p114) which is a combination of psychology and economics. Frame of reference is a critical thinking skill that has many applications both within the business world, education and many other disciplines.

- Managers can influence a buyer's perception of benefits and value. (Smith and Nagle).
- Business researchers have discovered that frames of reference can be used to influence consumers' perceptions of price and value
- Smith and Nagle have identified that "...there is a need to practice and understand how and why buyers respond to different ways of framing price, benefits and value." (p114)
- The use of framing in a business setting is "... grounded in 'prospect theory' ..." (Smith

and Nagle, p99). This is a combination of psychology and economics.

- Frames of Reference is a critical thinking skill that has many applications within the business world, education and several other disciplines.

Exercises for Frames of Reference

1. Name a company that makes computers. What influenced you to choose this particular computer company?

2. Name an accounting firm and identify what influenced you to choose this particular firm.

3. Name a temporary service and identify what influenced you to choose this particular service.

Identify the factors that influence your frames of reference:

Business Exercises

1. Explain how you could attempt to create a new reference point or frame of reference pertaining to the cost of an item.

2. Give an example of how your business could benefit by understanding "conflict frames"

3. A business has experienced a 10% price increase in a particular product. Using frames of reference, how could a business **reflect** a gain and avoid a loss to the customer. Or simply stated, how could a business use frames of reference to influence the customer to buy an item that now costs 10% more in price?

Methodological Believing

Methodological Believing is a critical thinking skill that involves a special type of role play. Using this skill, you adopt the other person's point of view and support it vigorously for a limited period of time - usually 5 minutes or less. During this time period you think of as many reasons as you can for supporting this position. You put yourself in the other person's shoes.

The purpose of this skill is to provide you with an understanding of an opposing point of view. Elbow (1986, p257) defines methodological believing as the "systematic, disciplined and conscious attempt [of believing] everything, no matter how unlikely, repellent it might seem ...." Once you have used this skill you will have a much better understanding of the opposing point of view. You'll be able to understand to a far greater degree why the opposing party thinks the way they do. You will be familiar with their frame of reference and be able to resolve disputes and conflicts easier by comprehending what is important to the opposition and why.

Methodological believing does require some practice. The easiest way to begin using this skill is to deliberately choose an opposing point of view. Once you've chosen it, write down on a sheet of paper all the reasons you can think of for supporting this position.

Let's start with the following past topic—the War in Iraq. Should we continue to stay there or pull out? Whatever you actually believe, take the opposing view and support it. Here are some examples.

Stay in Iraq	Pull Out
Finish the job, train Iraqis to defend their land	We've accomplished our goal. We toppled Hussein's government
Soldiers will die in vain if we pull out now	We've occupied the country long enough
Pulling out now will admit defeat	Iraq and other countries need to get involved
We must continue to fight terrorism	Enough of our troops have died there

The same technique can easily be applied to a business setting. Consider a classic management issue – use the authoritarian approach in managing or use a collaborative approach.

Authoritarian	Collaborative
Maintain tight control	Provide workers with more autonomy
Gets results	Increases creativity
Proven results, been around for long time	Fosters good morale and positive environment
Workers know what to do and when and how to do it	Encourages people to work to their potential

Now it's your turn—consider the opposing point of view and choose the one that you normally wouldn't support. Use Methodological Believing for five minutes and support that opposing position. Write down on a sheet of paper as many reasons as you can possibly identify for supporting the opposition.

Methodological believing is a skill that needs to be practiced, just like any other skill. Sometimes, after a person has used this skill, he actually changes his point of view and supports the opposing viewpoint. However, more often, you won't necessarily change your point of view, but will have a much clearer understanding about the opposing point of view. You may come to understand why someone thinks this way and what his frame of reference is. This information can help you to resolve conflicts and arrive at agreements. It can actually aide in negotiation.

Why Compromise is a Lose-Lose Proposition

The idea in using methodological believing is NOT to gain leverage and try to manipulate the opposition or even compromise. In a compromise, both parties lose something. They both concede something to revolve a conflict. Methodological believing provides you with a greater understanding of the other person's frame of reference. The question to ask is – how can we resolve this conflict and satisfy both parties? There is no guarantee that methodological believing will accomplish this. But, you will have a better understanding of what the opposition wants and why that is so important to them.

Synergy

When both parties genuinely want to resolve a conflict, sometimes it is possible to find a solution that is greater than the sum of the individual parts of the negotiation. Negotiation is an entire book in itself and way beyond the scope of this book. However, I emphasize that methodological believing can lead to creative solutions. I would like to suggest one simple action you can do in negotiation. – have both parties sit on the same side of the table. Rather than opposing each other, you sit on the same side and work together towards resolution. It doesn't always work, but neither does negotiation. Some conflicts can only be resolved with time – lots of time.

Understanding and believing an opposing point of view can be difficult to do. Many people are more skilled at criticizing and finding "flaws or contradictions" (Elbow 1986, p251). Perhaps doubting is easier than believing since "doubt implies disagreement from action of holding back, while belief implies action" (Elbow, 1986, p256). In fact, "methodological doubt" (Elbow 1986, p261) is described as "systematic and crossover attempt to criticize everything (Elbow 1986, p261).

One of the difficulties with methodological believing is that "trying to believe someone we disagree with makes us feel vulnerable" (Elbow, 1986, p266). An individual usually feels uncomfortable when looking at or discovering something that is different from one's perspective (Sargent 1984)). "Distress" is defined by Selye as anything that is uncomfortable (Selye, 1974). When you try to use methodological believing, initially you may feel uncomfortable, especially if you have strong feelings about the particular issue.

In my critical thinking classes, I often introduce a fairly low level, non-controversial issue, initially. An exercise I frequently use is the issue of civil disobedience. I have my students read an excerpt from Thoreau's Civil Disobedience and have them use methodological believing to address the question of is it ever okay to break the law? I then move into more controversial topics such as the death penalty or abortion. Such topics present a real challenge because they are so emotionally charged for most people.

Another difficulty with methodological believing is egocentric thinking, which is the tendency to view everything in relationship to oneself (Paul, 1990, 548). Ironically, methodological believing is the antithesis of egocentric thinking, because it promotes an awareness and willingness to view all points of view – despite one's feelings or personal interests (Paul, 1990, p198).

Despite the challenges methodological believing presents, it is an extremely valuable skill. It enables you to not only see the other side, but actually temporarily adopt the opposing point of view. Instead of "putting on the other person's shoes" you are "getting into their head". In fact, Elbow states, "give me the view in your head. You are having an experience I don't have. Help me to have it" (Elbow, 1986, p261)

In order to successfully use this skill, you need to be able to adopt the opposing point of view and realize that you're only doing this for a limited period of time (5 minutes). What you're really trying to do is find as many reasons as possible to support this position. Imagine you're an attorney and you must defend a position that you personally oppose. But, as a professional, you are obligated, even required to defend this position. Therefore, you need to know every possible reason for supporting this view point. You don't have to agree with it, But your goal is to better understand it. Why would someone think like this? What would their frame of reference be? What's important to them and why? The answers to some of these questions are what you will learn by using methodological believing. You must "look for favorable evidences and reason to support the belief in question." (Elbow, 1988, p276).

Methodological Believing, or the "believing game" as it is sometimes called, does have some rules. The basic one is the 5 minute time limit. Another rule or more of a suggestion is to look for something that is interesting or helpful about the viewpoint. As I've described earlier, it's best to practice this skill initially with a non-controversial issue. If you're a manager or supervisor, be advised that what you consider to be non-controversial could be a significant issue to others. It's best to check first with other people before attempting to use it.

For Managers

A good manager knows how to motivate employees and get the best effort and work from employees. All too often, when a manager has a "problem worker", a person who is not adequately performing his or her responsibilities, the manager, after speaking with the problem worker, will begin building a case for termination. While such action may be necessary, it might be more beneficial for the manager to use some methodological believing to understand the problem worker – especially if there is a conflict or opposing point of view. I am NOT talking about an employee who is disrespectful, defiant and/or seems to be deliberately being difficult or is breaking company policy. By using Methodological Believing, it may be possible to understand the problem worker's point of view. It's all too easy to simply terminate an employer. However, think of the time involved in recruiting, hiring, and training a new employee. Methodological Believing provides you with a way of understanding an opposing view – of understanding what is important to that employee and why. This skill provides managers with a specific way to accomplish this – to gain a better understanding of individual points of view that are in opposition to yours. This can be a very valuable skill.

Summary:

- Methodological believing is a powerful critical thinking skill that enables you to understand an opposing point of view.

- For a limited period of time (5 minutes), you adopt the opposing point of view and vigorously support it.

- The technique requires practice and presents a real challenge because initially it can cause you to feel vulnerable or uncomfortable.

- If you have very strong feelings about the issue and/or are polarized, this skill can be difficult to use.
- If done properly, you will gain much understanding of your opposition's point of view. This could lead to improved possibilities for resolving a conflict or negotiating a settlement.

Role-Playing Exercises for Methodological Believing

Remember, Methodological Believing is a special type of role play. For example, Thoreau stated in his book on Civil Disobedience "If the injustice...is of such a nature that it requires you to be the agent of injustice to another, then, I say, break the law."

This is a special type of role play where you take the opposite point of view and vigorously support it for a limited period of time – usually 5 minutes or less. This is a skill that requires practice. However, learning how to use this skill can be very beneficial. You can gain a much greater understanding about an adversary's position—understand why someone would think this way.

It is best to begin with something that you is not emotional laden or something that you have strong opinions about that could influence your decision.

TO DO:

In each exercise you will adapt the opposing point of view and argue for that position, passionately. While it is more effective to do these exercises with a partner, they can be done alone.

Whatever you believe—take the opposite position. Then use Methodological Believing and defend that position vigorously for a few minutes. Think of all the reasons you can to support this position. It's best to do this with a partner—each of you taking the opposite position of what you actually believe. However, you can do this exercise yourself.

After you've done some Methodological Believing, do some metacognition and think about your thinking.

Methodological Believing Exercise #1

Using the following business scenario, pick a position that is opposite of what you believe and use Methodological Believing.

Employees in a large business are demanding a raise. There's no union, but workers are entertaining the idea of getting organized and joining a union. Management's position is there's not enough money in the budget to give a raise to the workers. The Company does NOT want the workers to become unionized.

For 5 minutes, use Methodological Believing to support the opposite position of whatever you believe. Vigorously defend this position and think of as many reasons as you can to support it.

After you've done this exercise, answer these questions:

- Do you have a clearer understanding of the opposite position?
- Can you understand why someone would support such a position?
- Are any of the reasons on either side really valid?

Methodological Believing Exercise #2

A conflict has developed between management and employees. Management wants to institute a time clock punch in procedure, requiring employees to have their time card stamped by the clock. Currently, employees must get the signature of their supervisor.

If you are in favor of time cards being stamped by a clock, argue for the opposite position. If you're against time cards being stamped by a clock, argue for it.

Methodological Believing Exercise #3

Your business does not have a social media site. If you are for such a site, argue against it. If you are against having such a site, argue for it.

Methodological Believing Exercise #4

A manager refused to gave a customer a refund on a defective product because the customer was two days late in bringing the merchandise back to the store. The Company has a 30 day return policy. If you think the customer should be given a refund, argue for the Manager. If you agree with the Manager, argue for the customer.

Methodological Believing Exercise #5

A business has a strict policy about employees using the Internet for personal use. It is forbidden and all employees were given a written statement warning them that any employee caught using the Internet for non-business activity will be terminated. Jack is one of the lead sales people. He was caught checking his personal email account. If you believe Jack should be fire, argue for keeping him. If you believe Jack should be allowed to stay, argue for firing him.

Methodological Believing Exercise #6

A customer wrote a very negative post on the Company's business page on Facebook because three times he went to the store to buy a pair of shoes that were on sale. But each time only the more expensive shoes were available. He asked if he could purchase the more expensive shoes for the sales price and was denied that request.

If you think the customer should be granted his request, argue for the Company. If you think the Company was right in refusing his request, argue for the customer.

Now that you have had a chance to practice using this skill – think of ways you might actually apply it in your business. List at least 6 situations where Methodological Believing would help you to understand an adversary's position.

1.

2.

3.

4.

5.

Pick one of the above situations and create your own Methodological Believing exercises.

Practice Methodological Believing with a co-worker. Remember, each of you will actually support a point of view that you oppose. You might want to first make a list of points to cover and then passionate argue each point aloud to each other. Initially, pick a topic that is not emotionally charged.

To learn more about the "Believing Game go to:
http://www.esrnational.org/believinggame.htm

For further information about Methodological Believing read the web article on it at teachablemoment.org/high/criticalthinking.html

Causal Reasoning

What is Causal Reasoning? How is it used in business? What are its limitations?

Causal reasoning is often referred to as cause and effect reasoning. This type of reasoning seeks to find and explain relationships between two objects or two events. The basic theory is that X causes Y to happen. Here's an example: Attendance of employees at a particular business was up for the month of July. Using cause and effect reasoning, you would attempt to find out why this happened. What caused attendance to improve during the month of July? This type of reasoning is sometimes called inductive reasoning.

Another form of reasoning is called deductive. This type of reasoning is often used in courts and legal cases. It's based upon logic and results in specific conclusion. But, it is not always correct – although the argument might be sound. If the basic premise is wrong, the conclusion may be wrong as well. Here's an example: If it's raining the sidewalk will be wet. The sidewalk is wet, therefore it's raining. The first statement, called a premise, is flawed. There could be several reasons why the sidewalk is wet beside from rain.

I mentioned deductive and inductive reasoning because they are both types of reasoning that could be using in a cause and effect argument. More often, however, people seek an explanation for what has happened – a cause for the effect. The problem with this type of reasoning is that you can come to the wrong conclusion. You might find that what you believe to be a cause and effect relationship is incorrect!

Causal reasoning seeks to find and explain relationships between two objects or two events.

Oftentimes a chain reaction can result. You think you've identified the cause of an effect. You attempt to take action which results in another effect. Here's an example: A sales manager notices that sales were down during the month of August. She believes the cause of this is the weather. It's been very hot and humid and she figures that the sales force is reluctant to go out in the field and make sales calls because of the heat, when they could remain in a comfortable air-conditioned office. Now she can't control the weather, but she could try and motivate her staff with some incentives to balance the elements. She introduces a bonus incentive and offers a prize to whoever makes the most sales for the week. But, what if the weather is not the real cause of the drop in sales?

The following month she introduces the new bonus plan. This month, September, the temperature drops and it's not as hot. Much to her surprise, sales have not improved! Now her profits are even lower because of her new bonus plan and sales still haven't improved.

When you use causal reasoning, you must use some other critical thinking skills as well. You must check for assumptions and challenge them. In the

90

above example, the sales manager assumed she knew the cause for the drop in sales. Her assumptions proved wrong and cost the company more money. You might also need to check on your frame of reference.

Oftentimes causal reasoning is based upon what someone thinks or believes. This is where critical thinking becomes essential. You must seek evidence for your thoughts or beliefs. While you may believe something, that doesn't mean that it is true.

Consider the following scenario: A speaker was giving a presentation using a hand held microphone. Whenever he walked near a plant that was on the stage, the microphone starting producing feedback. After this happened 2-3 times, the audience became convinced that the plant was somehow causing the feedback. A plant sitting in dirt in a plastic container cannot product any type of feedback. Yet, people became convinced that there was a cause and effect relationship between the plant and the feedback. Some of the members of the audience actually began yelling that it was the plant causing the feedback! (According to Anthony Robbins Personal Power Tapes) Of course, it wasn't the plant, but the example clearly demonstrates how cause and effect thinking can be flawed.

In a business setting, flawed thinking can be costly. Yet, how many decisions are based on cause and effect reasoning? It's not wrong to use cause and effect reasoning. It can be very useful to identify what is causing the problem – the effect. But, oftentimes such reasoning requires the use of other critical thinking skills such as identifying and challenging assumptions, seeking evidence and, sometimes, identifying one's frame of reference.

How often has your business used cause and effect reasoning? How often have you personally, used it in business? In the business world it can be difficult to document and prove that a genuine cause and effect relationship exists. While it may take time to look for such a relationship, it is important to carefully examine and qualify the information to determine if such a relationship exists.

Summary

- Causal reasoning is often referred to as cause and effect.
- Sometimes the cause of an effect is not readily apparent.
- When you use causal reasoning, you must use some other critical thinking skills such as checking for assumptions and identifying your frame of reference.
- Oftentimes causal reasoning is based upon what someone thinks or believes.
- When using causal reasoning it is important to carefully examine and qualify the information.

Exercises for
Causal Reasoning

Let's look at some business cause and effect relationships:

1. An increase in sales causes profit to rise.

2. State of the art computers result in increasing office productions.

3. A good marketing plan causes an increase in sales.

4. Close supervision of workers causes them to be more productive.

Now, examine each statement and use several critical thinking skills. For example, examine statement #1 to see how causal reasoning could be applied:

#1. *An increase in sales causes profits to increase.* Is this statement true? The answer is – maybe. It depends on what items are being sold. If high price items decline in sales, but low price items increase, profits might actually fall. If a computer store is selling mostly accessories, such as blank cd's diskettes, etc. but very few computer systems, then profits probably will fall, not increase.

As a critical thinker you must analyze and question information. With the first example, a question to ask is *What type of sales?* Without knowing the type of sales, the cause and effect relationship may be false. In the business world it can be difficult to document and prove that a genuine cause and effect relationship exists. It's not a waste of time to look for such a relationship. But it is important to carefully examine and qualify the information.

TO DO:

Carefully analyze each statement. Determine as best you can if the cause and effect relationship is genuine – if it's really true. Seek evidence to prove it or disprove it. If possible, collaborate with a partner.

2. State of the art computers result in increasing office productions.

3. A good marketing plan causes an increase in sales.

4. Close supervision of workers causes them to be more productive

More To Do:

Identify some of your own conclusions regarding cause and effect. Analyze them. Examine cause and effect relationships that you are aware of at your place of employment. Determine if they are true or not.

Make a list of other critical thinking skills to use to help you examine cause and effect relationships.

Include some questions to ask such as, *How do I know that this is true?*

Have you made decisions based upon cause and effect reasoning? How have these decisions impacted upon your workplace?

Additional Cause and Effect Practice Exercises

Determine if each statement demonstrated a cause and effect relationship. Did one event cause another?

- You flip a light switch and the light goes on.
- A lecturer speaking on a stage, keeps getting feedback when he walks near a plant that is on stage.
- At the exact moment a man turned on his cold water faucet a plane flew over head and the faucet broke.
- An IT specialist went to a conference about computer security. The next day he found a virus on his computer system.
- Susan doesn't have any virus protection on her computer and she keeps getting viruses on it.
- Shawn just started learning how to play the clarinet. Each time he plays a certain note, the clarinet squeaks. Shawn is convinced that he has a defective clarinet.
- An employee who receives average annual review got stung by a bee. After that incident his review dramatically improved.

- When Luis moves the mouse connected to his computer an "I beam" on the screen corresponds to the mouse movement.
- Gary works on the first floor of a two story building. When he goes into the storage room he hears a low pitched motor but can't find the source of the noise. A friend of his who believes in ghosts tell him that the building is haunted and that the noise is caused by a ghost.
- Whenever Jane turns on her a top burner on her gas stove, a flame goes on.
- When Ben opens the refrigerator door at the office, a light goes on.
- When you press a button to let someone in, you hear a buzzing sound.
- Whenever Marie drives over a bridge she says, "here we go" and that allows her to safely cross a bridge.
- Carlos moved some heavy office furniture and strained a muscle in his arm. Whenever he presses on it, it hurts more.
- Whenever Andre whistles for his dog, his dog comes running to him.
- A man's dog bit him. The man thinks his dog bit him because the dog was hungry.
- Every time Bob uses the copying machine, the lights in the room dim.
- Whenever Jamie eats wheat he feels ill. But when he doesn't eat wheat, he feels fine.
- Whenever Dennis uses a new razor blade he cuts himself.

- A black cat crossed Sally's path while she was going for a job interview. She got the job! Sally now believes a black cat crossing her path brought her good luck.

Now it is your turn. Create some statements that demonstrate cause and effect.

1.

2.

3.

4.

5.

Now create some statement that do not demonstrate a cause and effect relationshio.

1.

2

3

4

5

Metacognition

Metacognition means thinking about your thinking. Some people consider this skill to be the granddaddy of critical thinking skills because it involves several other critical thinking skills already discussed, including identifying and challenging assumptions, frames of reference, asking questions and more.

Initially some business people fail to understand how this skill can be applied in a business setting. In my opinion, it is one of the most valuable critical thinking skills.

How to Use It

Managers in particular are often confronted with decisions to make. Good managers use critical thinking to make these decisions. They seek evidence and challenge assumptions. However, there is so much more managers can do to improve their decision making skills. Thinking about your thinking will help you to identify your own biases, assumptions and frames of reference, By using metacognition, you can learn to ask yourself important questions that will help you to gain clarity and make better decisions affecting your business.

Consider the story I told earlier about the manager who had a bad experience with noxious chemicals and rejected a new copier because it had been set up in a small room with inadequate ventilation. The manager rejected the copier despite the fact that it was a great machine and was offered at a great price. Had this manager engaged in metacognition, she probably would have been able to identify that her previous bad experience with noxious odors was influencing her decision about buying this equipment – which was really needed.

Thinking about one's thinking does not usually occur naturally. This is a skill that needs to be learned and practiced – and I emphasize **practiced**. When you think about your thinking you begin to closely examine how and why you do what you do. This can be extremely valuable information. You can learn a lot about how you think and act by paying attention to your thinking. Often a good place to start is with a simple decision. It's amazing what you can discover about yourself.

Consider the following scenario: It's lunch time and you have to decide where to go for lunch. You are currently at work. You enjoy eating pizza, so you decide that's what you you'd like to eat today. Now the question is – Where do you go to get the pizza? You could call Dominos' Pizza, which is known for their fast delivery service. But you don't really care for the taste of Domino's Pizza. You could go to the Italian Restaurant down the street, but it's often crowded at lunch time. If you wanted to travel a few more blocks, you could get a pizza at a local eatery – a pretty good quality at a decent price. If you're really in a hurry, you can drive a couple of miles and get a few slices of pizza from the supermarket. The pizza is good, but the ambience leaves a lot to be desired.

As you can see, there are several possibilities and you haven't even considered the type of pizza you want. Do you want just cheese? How about some veggies? Or do you like pepperoni? What about a pizza with chicken? Do you prefer whole wheat or just regular dough? Are some pizzas more greasy than others? Are you concerned about your weight and/or cholesterol? What about trans-fat?

There are a lot of things to consider and choices to be made. Perhaps you're unaware about all of these thoughts, and usually just order some pizza from the same place all the time. As you continue to 'think about your thinking', you might identify that you often make decisions based upon what you usually do. While this certainly saves you time, is it the best decision?

Thus far I've only been talking about a somewhat routine and simple decision – ordering a pizza. Suppose you now focus on buying some office supplies. Do you simply re-order whatever you've been using from the same merchant, or do you consider other possibilities? Expand this concept further. Do you often make decisions based upon what you already know, or do you consider other facts and information. If you responded to this question by saying it depends, I would ask, "It depends on what?"

As you begin to think about your thinking you can discover all sorts of information about how you think, what influences your decisions and what patterns of thinking you use. You can even use metacognition to determine how you interact with people. It's helpful to think about your thinking if you always seem to get into an argument or disagreement with a particular employee. What are you thinking? Why does this always happen with this particular employee and not with others? As you use metacognition, you can begin to analyze your thinking and perhaps discover why the scenario is repeated frequently.

The more important a decision, the more important it is to use metacognition. Like any other skill, metacognition requires practice. It's best to start with some small, relatively unimportant decisions and think about your thinking with minor types of decisions before attempting to use metacognition with an important decision.

Oftentimes you will want to consider other critical thinking skills, including frame of reference, identifying and challenging assumptions, examining the cause and effect relationship. When you engage in metacognition, you may find yourself using several critical thinking skills.

Another important time to use metacognition is when you feel yourself getting upset. This is an ideal time to stop whatever it is you are doing, take a deep breath and begin thinking about your thinking. Emotions can greatly influence your thoughts. If you can step back from whatever you are doing and think about your thinking, you may make some valuable discoveries about your thinking. (The relationship between stress and critical thinking will be discussed in another chapter). You will probably discover that your thinking changes considerably when you are stressed. It may be fine to have an outward appearance of calmness. However, if you feel distressed (uncomfortable) in any way, including feeling annoyed, nervous, anxious, threatened, worried, etc. such distress will affect your thinking. This is really the time to use metacognition to learn how you think when you are under stress. If you think you function the same way under stress as you do when you're not distressed, you are deceiving yourself.

The use of metacognition could have profound effects upon problem solving, education, business and industry. Teachers could learn a great deal about how their students think by having them do some metacognition, especially when the student gives a wrong answer. Teachers could actually have their students examine their thinking process by asking them such questions as "what makes you think that?" or "what evidence do you have to support that idea?" Within the area of science and math, metacognition can be extremely helpful in helping a student to discover where he or she "went wrong". Rather than simply teaching students to memorize a math formula, students could begin to actually see where they erred by thinking about their thinking.

The application of metacognition in the business world could also produce significant changes by having workers think about their thinking and discover why they are thinking the way they are. Assumptions, biases, and frames of reference could be discovered by workers who engage in metacognition. Managers and supervisors can promote critical thinking by asking questions that enable employees to examine their thinking. The same questions that could be asked by teachers could also be asked in the business world.

Industry and the scientific community could also benefit by using metacognition. A team of scientists or engineers working together on a project could explain their thinking to each other and truly work together in a collaborative nature.

The use of metacognition is yours to chose whenever you wish. It's best to practice this skill with low risk, unimportant decisions, first, before progressing to more important ones. Thinking about your thinking requires mental effort and some discipline.

Summary:

- Metacognition means thinking about your thinking
- Thinking about your thinking requires mental effort, practice and discipline.
- It is best to practice this skill first when you are not under pressure and the decision to be made is not very important. As you gain more competency, progress to more difficult and important decisions
- Distress interferes with thinking.

Thinking about your thinking oftentimes involves other critical thinking skills including identifying and challenging assumptions, frames of reference and other thinking skills.

Exercises for Metacognition

To further help you develop this skill, please complete the following exercises.

List in order of importance. (Note: there is no "right" or "wrong" answer). Rank order each set of items. Then provide reasons why you chose this particular order.

Each of these rank orders will require you to make a decision and identify the reason(s) for your decision. As you do these exercises, be on the lookout for your assumptions, frames of reference, etc. Why do you think what you do? Is it based upon a fact or an assumption? Is this simply a belief? Think about your thinking!

1. fruit, vegetable mineral

2. magazine, newspaper, book

3. scissors, stapler, ruler

4. voice mail, US mail, email

5. marketing, accounting, sales.

More To Do:

For each item, decide where you would purchase it and why.

Item	Business Chosen	Reasons
Office supplies		
Printer		
Copier		
Flowers		

Decision Making

Consider the following decisions to be made and use metacognition in arriving at your decision.

1. A dress code

2. New office policy

3. Late policy

4. No smoking policy – anywhere on the premises – even outside the building

Further Exercises on Metacognition:

Metacognition means "thinking about one's thinking". As you use this technique you will begin to discover assumptions, frames of reference and errors or fallacies in your thinking. One of the best ways to practice this technique is to attempt to solve a problem and pay careful attention to what you are thinking.

Problems – the goal is to use Metacognition. If you solve the problem, that's a bonus.

1. A man has a chicken, a dog and a bag of grain which he must transport across a river. He has a tiny boat. If he leaves the dog with the chicken, the dog will eat the chicken. If he leaves the chicken with the grain, the chicken will eat the grain. How does he get all three across the river? (The origins of this puzzle are unknown).

- In attempting to solve this problem, did you make any assumptions?
- Did you use any frames of reference (such as "I never was good at solving these types of problems")?
- Were you assumptions and frames of reference helpful or a hindrance?
- Did you notice any flaws or errors in your thinking – such as thinking something that illogical or out of sequence?

- Did you use a particular strategy in attempting to solve this puzzle and do you usually use such a strategy.
- Did you notice any patterns about how you were thinking that you use in other areas as well. Are they useful or a hindrance?
- Did you discover any flaws or biases in your thinking?

2. "Copy and Paste" is a very useful word processing technique. The procedure is as follows:

- highlight the text to be copied.
- Go to Edit and choose "copy"
- Place the cursor where you want copied text to appear.
- Go to Edit and choose "paste"

A) Many beginners can't seem to get this to work. Nothing happens when they choose "paste". What are they doing wrong? (Refer to the above questions as you try and solve this problem). Even if you don't use a computer – attempt to solve the problem and refer to the above questions).

B) Another problem that beginners experience is the copied text appears right after what they've typed or it may even appear in the middle of what they typed. As you attempt to solve this problem, refer to the questions above.

Rectangle Problem

- Part A— remove 3 lines and get 4 rectangles.
- Part B— remove 4 line and get 3 rectangles.

Refer to the questions listed below.

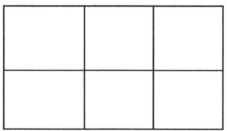

Remember— the purpose of this exercise is to think about your thinking.

- In attempting to solve this problem, did you make any assumptions?
- Did you use any frames of reference (such as I never was good at solving these types of problems)?
- Were you assumptions and frames of reference helpful or a hindrance?
- Did you notice any flaws or errors in your thinking – such as thinking something that illogical or out of sequence?
- Did you use a particular strategy in attempting to solve this puzzle and do you usually use such a strategy.
- Did you notice any patterns about how you were thinking that you use in other areas as well. Are they useful or a hindrance?

Team Building Problem

At a workshop on Team Building, four participants were given the task of walking across the room, but each person had to have a a "pass" in their hand in order to cross the room. They were only given one pass and with the following restrictions.

- They couldn't throw, toss or slide the pass from one person to another.
- They couldn't create another pass
- All four people has to have a pass in their hand in order to cross the room.

Please refer to the questions above when attempting to solve this problem.

Rank the following in order of importance. Then "think about your thinking" and identify why you chose that order. (There is no "right" or "wrong" answer).

1. tablet, cell phone and a laptop.

After you have chosen an order for the above, identify why you chose the order you did. Recall any frames of reference or assumptions. Explain your thinking. Why did you choose this order?

2. computer, copier, phone.

Again, explain your thinking. Why did you choose this order? Did you make any assumptions or use any frames or reference?

3. copy machine, fax machine overhead projector.

Again, explain your thinking. Why did you choose this order? Did you make any assumptions or use any frames of reference?

4. purchase order, receipt, inventory list.

Why did you choose this order? Did you make any assumptions or use any frames of reference?

5. pencil, eraser, straight edge.

Why did you choose this order? Did you make any assumptions or use any frames of reference?

6. sales report, inventory report, accounting report.

Explain why you chose this order. Note any assumptions you made or any frames of reference.

METACOGNITION as a training or teaching technique.

Metacognition can also be used as a training or teaching technique. This is especially useful when there is a process or procedure required. Here are just a few examples:

- a technician doing a service call
- a sales person making a sales call
- a factory worker using a machine
- Human Resources selecting a candidate for employment

In each of these situations, there is a process or procedure involved. When the task is completed, if you ask the person how they arrived at their decision, they will tell you. In essence, what they are doing is "thinking about their thinking" as they go over each step of the process or procedure.

By asking someone how they arrived at their conclusion, you are in effect, asking them to use Metacognition and "think about their thinking".

Now it's your turn. Identify a process or procedure you use. Describe it and list all the steps involved. After you have done this:

check and make sure you didn't omit any required step

Notice if you are using any Frames of Reference or making any assumptions.

If you omitted any step, determine how this happened by asking yourself these questions and answering them:

- Did you omit this step because you never learned it?
- Did you omit this step because you forgot it?
- Did you make any assumptions?
- Did you use any Frames of Reference?
- Did you find any other flaws in your thinking?
- Are you more aware of your thinking and is this helpful to you? Explain.

Using Metacognition as a Training Technique

Do you teach or train employees about some procedure? You can quickly determine how well an individual understands a particular process. This is especially useful for service people/technicians or anyone that engages in a process. Simply ask them - how did they arrived at their conclusion?

Whenever there is a series of steps involved, it's important for employees to know each of those steps. By asking them how they arrived at their conclusion they will tell you and you will immediately see if they are missing some information or have a comprehensive understanding of the series of steps or process.

114

What you will be doing is actually getting them to use Metacognition – to think about their thinking.

Identify people in your Company who engage in a process or must know a series of steps to take.

List people in those positions:

-
-
-
-
-

If you are responsible for training or teaching these employees, have them do some metacognition. Ask then how they arrived at their conclusion.

Stress and Critical Thinking

There's a strong relationship between stress and critical thinking. A little bit of stress is actually motivating, but too much stress (distress) becomes uncomfortable and is a problem. Sargent (1984) states that distress "impairs awareness" and defines awareness as "the capacity to experience consciously" (p46). When individuals are under stress, their attention and awareness become restricted.

However, the problem that distress presents is far more encompassing. Not only is awareness impaired, but there is an increased rigidity in thinking that results in regressive behavior (Sargent 1984). As Sargent states:

> This happens first through loss of cognitive flexibility. Then as stress further increases, the nature of the rigidity itself begins to change. Earlier and more firmly entrenched behaviors begin to be observed. (p7).

As a person becomes more stressed, awareness restricts, thinking becomes rigid and the individual resorts to earlier learned patterns of coping. The response to distress is what Sargent (1984) calls "automatic" and "usually does not take place under the individual's control." (p11). This is a prescription for disaster when making an important business decision.

If thinking is difficult when one is stressed, critical thinking is all but impossible.

There are many definitions of critical thinking. Ennis defines it as "reasonable reflective thinking that is focused on decided what to believe or do" (Ennis 1987, p10). It's worth mentioning again that if it's difficult to think when one is distressed, it is nearly impossible to think critically when distressed. Janis (1982) states that "stress reduces the decision maker's problem solving capabilities" (p70). The following description provides a good summary of some of the effects of distress upon critical thinking.

"The person's attention and perceptions are somewhat impaired and there are various manifestations of cognitive rigidity. These cognitive deficiencies result in narrowing the range of the perceived alternative, overlooking long-term consequences, inefficient searching for information, erroneous assessing of expected outcomes ...." (Janis 1982, p70)

Oftentimes in business, problem solving is necessary. Mandler (1982) states that in problem solving the "thought processes become narrowed in the sense that only obvious alternatives are considered" (p102). Meichenbaum (1983), another researcher of stress, claims that under "undue stress, the individual's cognitive ability (problem solving, memory, ability to focus attention) may be negatively affected as well" (p64). When people get distressed, they become "distracted and their train of thought gets derailed" (Janis 1982, p77). They are likely to become obsessed and dwell upon "the worst possible outcomes" (Janis 1982, p77).

It's clear that distress can have a devastating effect upon thinking and especially critical thinking. Ironically, it's when we really need clarity to make an important decision that many of us become distressed and make the worst possible decision. This compounds the problem and makes things worse and adds to the person's stress. Especially, when there's a lot at stake (money and one's career), decision making can be very stressful. Therefore, it becomes essential to have some skill at lowering one's stress level. While there are many different definitions of stress, it is largely a subjective perception. If you feel that something is stressful, it is to you. But what is stressful for some people can be a source of pleasure for others. Many people dread public speaking. Some are actually terrified of it. Yet, for some people, like myself, I really enjoy it. It's important to realize that what is stressful for some people may actually be a source of joy for others. Unfortunately, job responsibilities often include tasks that are stressful or, at the least, unpleasant.

Fortunately, there are several different ways of managing stress. The more well known techniques include meditation and relaxation. But these techniques, although effective require time to develop and aren't always practical to do in a work setting.

If everyone could take 20 minutes from their work schedule and go and meditate or relax, the work environment would probably improve significantly and so would production.

> **Recent Pleasant Experience (RPE):**
> identify anything that recently occurred that made you feel "good."
> Some people even keep a journal for RPEs.

Therefore, I'd like to introduce you to a few techniques that you can do right on the job. The first technique I want to describe I call **Recent Pleasant Experience** (RPE). To do this you identify something you have recently experienced that made you feel "good". It can be something as simple as enjoying a new breakfast cereal to something more like winning the lottery. The important thing is to identify anything that recently occurred that made you feel "good" (meaning not distressed). The technique is an excellent way to begin a business meeting. Each person shares a Recent Pleasant Experience. This enhances a positive mood and helps relax people. I would allow people to "pass" if they can't identify any Recent Pleasant Experience. However, for those people who can't identify any Recent Pleasant Experience, perhaps they can identify a Past Pleasant Experience – something that happened last week or last month or a few months ago. Finally, if someone can't even identity a pleasant experience from the past, I would then ask, "What's the least bad thing that has happened to you lately". This will usually produce a chuckle and enable the individual to identify a Recent Pleasant Experience.

Because this is a "portable technique", it does not require any special equipment and can be done anywhere. Some suggested uses of this technique include anytime you are waiting for an appointment, stuck in traffic or right after an unpleasant interaction.

120

Don't underestimate the effects of this technique. While it is simple to describe and do, it is not so simple to explain how it works. Suffice it to say that this technique forces you to think and move out of distress rather than remain in a stew of distressing thoughts and feelings.

One final comment regarding the Recent Pleasant Experience technique. It is best to practice this technique when you are NOT distressed. Some people actually keep a journal and record the RPEs each day. The more stress you are experiencing the more difficult it will be to identify a Recent Pleasant Experience. Therefore you can use this technique to gauge how much stress you are experiencing.

Another technique I recommend for the workplace is **Skimming**. Using this technique, you first pick an emotional state that you would like to experience – i.e. relaxation. Then you think of all the times or places you have actually felt relaxed. The idea is to "skim" the surface because if you focus too much on any one particular place or time, you are likely to also surface some distress.

This is another "portable" technique – one you can do anywhere at anytime. You can "skim" any desired feeling including feeling calm, joy, peaceful, confident, appreciated, etc. This technique can be used before or after a distressing event. Take a few minutes during your day to "skim" some pleasant memories.

Both of these techniques are "cognitive/affective" techniques, meaning that they affect thinking and feeling. A thought can trigger a feeling.

If you're about to make an important decision, you can't afford to make a mistake because of stress. With a bit of practice you can become very proficient using these techniques which will improve your ability to think critically, solve problems and make decisions.

Oftentimes, when we're under pressure (stress) we make poor decisions. Later, some of us will berate ourselves for making such a poor decision. Have you ever found yourself saying such things to yourself as "I'm stupid." "How could I be so dumb?" "I can't do anything right." These invalidating statements are not helpful and are oftentimes triggered in times of stress. To counteract such statements, it is useful to focus on your accomplishments – what you've done right or the times you've been successful. This is actually another stress reducing technique called validation or simply taking time to appreciate what you do well.

Summary

- When stress becomes uncomfortable it is called 'distress'.
- Distress impairs thinking and makes critical thinking nearly impossible.
- There are number of "portable skills" that you can use to reduce stress. These skills include Recent Pleasant Experiences and Skimming
- In times of stress many people say invalidating statements about themselves. A way to counteract such action is to focus on one's accomplishments or successes.

- Validation is a stress reducing technique where one focuses upon one's accomplishments or successes rather than focusing upon a poor decision made while under stress.

Exercises for Stress & Critical Thinking

EFFECTS OF DISTRESS

Distress distorts perception. Note a time that your perception was distorted when you were distressed

Distress impairs thinking. Note a time you had difficulty thinking when you were distressed.

Distress triggers automatic responses (habits). Note a time when you were distressed and automatically responded/reacted.

Note any difficulty in doing this activity. It is quite common for people to have difficulty doing this activity. As you think about a distressing time, you begin to experience distress and its effect upon your perception, thinking and behavior. Imagine what happens if you try to think critically when you're distressed. (Adapted from Sargent, 1984)

Recent Pleasant Experience (RPE)

Here's a technique you can do right in the workplace. This is a simple, yet effective technique to reduce distress. Identify anything that you recently experienced that was pleasant. It can be something little, like getting a call from a friend, or something big like getting a promotion or winning the lottery.

Identify some Recent Pleasant Experiences:

Past Pleasant Experiences - If you can't identify anything recent, pleasant experience, then identify some past pleasant experiences.

Finally, if you can't identify even a past pleasant experience, ask yourself this question: "What's the least bad thing that has happened to you recently". That will usually produce a chuckle and then you'll be able to identify a recent, pleasant experience.

Suggestion: Begin a meeting with everyone sharing a "**Recent Pleasant Experience**" (RPE). It begins the meeting on a real positive note and actually helps to energize people.

(adapted from Sargent, 1984)

More Stress Management Exercises

The Inventory – just as a retail store does an inventory of their stock, you can take an inventory of your positive qualities. This is something that can be done on an on-going basis.

Make a list of the positive qualities you use to do your job. It can be helpful to think of three specific categories: Strength, Skill and Talent.

Here are some examples of a training specialist

Strength	Skill	Talent
Oral presentation	Excellent listener	Humorous
Physical stamina	Highly organized	Creative
Persuasive writing	Flexible	Sensitive

Now it's your turn. Make a list of your strengths, skills and talents.

Strength	Skill	Talent

(Continue this exercise in a notebook and add to it each day)

How to use the Inventory.

Especially when you experience a "bad" day, when you make a mistake and are criticized for it or are dealing with unappreciative people, review your Inventory to reflect upon your positive qualities. Note that many people continue to criticize themselves, often worse than their worst critic. Now, you have an alternative to self criticism.

Keep a Journal

Another variation of the Inventory is to keep a journal of positive qualities about yourself. Each day enter one or two positive qualities about yourself into your journal.

Critical Thinking and Business Ethics

Ethics concern what we believe to be right. Sometimes "ethics" are called morals and pertain to what we believe is "right" or "proper". Morals or ethics are often tied to religious beliefs. There is a strong connection between critical thinking and business ethics (or any ethics for that matter).

Most businesses subscribe to a certain set of ethics. In large businesses or corporations, they often have a "mission statement" which identifies the purpose of the business and oftentimes outlines how that entity conducts business. Many non-profits also have a "mission statement".

The bottom line in most businesses is to make money. But the question arises, how to make money? This is where ethics become important, because there are many ways to make money. While most businesses offer a service or a product, it is how they offer this service or product that becomes important in regards to ethics.

There are many ways to make money ranging from running a completely honest business to engaging in criminal activities. A business may be legal, but that doesn't mean what they are doing is ethical.

Consider this scenario: A cabinet maker is approached by a large computer company. The computer company wants the cabinet maker to construct 10,000 cabinets to house a computer in each one. The cabinet maker, who knows little about computers, except how to run one is thrilled. But suppose that cabinet maker knows that computers placed in a cabinet, will overheat because they lack proper ventilation. Does the cabinet maker raise this issue with the computer company and risk losing the account? Here's where ethics enter into the decision.

It's easy to rationalize and claim, "hey, I'm just making cabinets. It's not my problem if the computers overheat". Another aspect on the dilemma is, if I raise this issue with the computer company, I could lose their business. Since I'm not breaking the law or doing any thing wrong, I'll just go ahead and make the cabinets. Anyway, a big computer company must know what they are doing".

Oftentimes, critical thinking is needed to sort out these types of dilemmas. Let's consider another scenario. A software salesman is selling a business product which is very comprehensive, but has a definite learning curve and takes several weeks to learn how to use the software. A customer is considering buying the product and asks the salesperson if it's difficult to learn how to use it. How the salesperson answers this question depends on his/her ethics. If the salesperson is honest, the question will be answered honestly. However, if the salesperson values the sale more than honesty, the likely response will be a dishonest answer, attempting to convince the customer that the

128

software is easy to learn how to use. A possible response from the salesperson might be, if you have average intelligence, you won't have any problem. This implies that if the customer does have a problem he/she must be below average in intelligence.

Is it wrong to make a statement like this? It isn't if you value a sale more than honesty. Whether that action is wrong depends upon your ethics or values and those of the Company where you are employed. Generally, over time, if you trick customers, they will stop buying from you and will spread the word to other potential customers as well. It may take a while, but eventually, sales will decline, leaving the sales manager wondering why.

I think you can begin to see the role that ethics play in business and how critical thinking is necessary to sort out some of these ethical dilemmas. Fortunately, once you have decided upon your ethics or morals there are some tests to determine what to do when you face an ethical dilemma. Oftentimes, the decision is not clear cut.

There are several ethical decision making tests that one can use in making difficult decisions. One is called the Role Exchange Test (Diestler 2001). Using this test you try to understand someone's frame of reference that is different from your own. The test attempts to have you empathize with people who will be affected by what you plan to do. You ask yourself such questions as: How would people affected by your decision feel and what consequences would they face? Would it be right for the other person to take this action if you were the one to experience the consequences of the decision?

> The Role Exchange Test: Try to understand someone's frame of reference that is different from your own. How would you feel?

This is similar to Methodological Believing where you adopt the opposing point of view. Using the Role Exchange Test, you imagine changing places with the person who would receive the effects of your decision and decide to "treat the other person as you would want to be treated in his or her place (Diestler 2001).

Here's an example. You see your friend's wife out with another man. You need to decide whether or not to tell your friend about his wife. You're reluctant to say anything because you know it would hurt him and you think it's really none of your business. But, when you do the Role Exchange Test, you decide to inform your friend because you realize that you would want to know if you were in his situation.

Another test is the Universal Consequences Test, which focuses on the "general results (consequences) of an action you might take" (Dietsler 2001). Using this test you "imagine what would happen if everyone in this situation similar to yours took this action" (Dietsler 2001 p44). Using this test, you determine if you would find it unacceptable for everyone in a similar situation to take this action..." (Dietsler 2001 p44). If you did find it unacceptable, then you would reject the action.

> **Universal Consequences Test**: "imagine what would happen if everyone in this situation similar to yours took this action"

Here's an example. You drain the radiator of your car and put in fresh anti-freeze. Now you have a bucket of used anti-freeze and wonder what to do with it. Driving to the recycle center is a nuisance when you could just dump it down the sewer. But, after realizing the consequences of everyone dumping anti-freeze down the sewer, rather than properly disposing of it at the recycle center, you decide to take it to the recycle center.

A similar situation could happen in an office where you change the toner of a copier and need to decide how to dispose of the older toner. Do you just throw it out with the trash or do you dispose of it separately. The New Cases Test has you consider if you action is consistent with other actions that are in the same category

The New Cases Test (described below) has you consider if your action is consistent with other actions that are in the same category. You choose the most difficult case you can and see if you would act the same way in that situation as you would in the current situation you are facing. If your answer is "yes", then your choice is consistent with your principles.

> **The New Cases Test**: consider if your action is consistent with other actions that are in the same category.

131

Here's an example. You're selling a software package and really need to make this sale. If you do, you'll receive a substantial bonus with an increased commission and an all expenses paid trip to the Bahamas. You believe in being honest and telling the customer the truth. The software package is difficult to learn and this fact usually influences that sale in a negative way. The customer asks you if the software is difficult to learn. Do you answer honestly and forfeit the extra commission and the trip or do you decide not to answer honestly? If you answer dishonestly, you might need to reconsider your principles.

The Higher Principles Test asks you to decide if the principle you're basing your action upon is consistent with a higher principle you accept (Diestler 2001). Here's an example. Your co-worker is not doing his share of maintaining the office. You find various office supplies all over the office even though he agreed to do so. None of the supplies are put back where they belong. You're tired of cleaning up after your co-worker and are considering doing the same thing. However, you value promises and integrity and you both agreed to keep the office in order. You decide to keep doing your share of putting supplies away and talk with your co-worker about the situation.

In the business world one frequently finds oneself in situations where one's ethics are called into question. These tests offer you a way of determining

---

The Higher Principles Test: asks you to decide if the principle you're basing your action upon is consistent with a higher principle you accept.

---

what is the correct action, based upon your values or ethics. An action can be legal but not ethical. It's also possible for an action to be illegal but still ethical. Consider this scenario. Tim works for the educational division of a large company. He's responsible for producing a catalog of the various courses the Company is offering. Tim's under pressure to get this catalog published. He finds some course descriptions written by an instructor and decides to use them in the catalog. The catalog is published and everyone is pleased with Tim's work.

A few weeks later, Tim's supervisor gets a call from the former instructor who claims the Company plagiarized his material. If this had been an actual classroom situation, there would be serious consequences. But plagiarism, while unethical isn't necessarily illegal. If the material had been copyrighted by the instructor, then the action would have been illegal.

Whether or not there is a copyright violation depends on a few circumstances. First, it's important to be aware that, since 1989, an author is not required to register a copyright or put a notice on the work. Current copyright law in the United States holds that a work is under copyright protection by virtue of being in physical tangible form, including computer files. A company, rather than the author may own the copyright if the work was done "for hire," that is the author was paid by the company to produce the work. Works published prior to 1923 are out of copyright, and into the "Public Domain." After 1923 but before 1989, the status is more complex to determine as it depends on whether there was a copyright notice on the original publication and whether the copyright was registered and renewed. For more detail, see the information at the Library of Congress Copyright office, or the summary by Banis, 2001.

Even if a work is out of copyright, and it is legal to copy and modify it, it is probably not ethical to do so without crediting the original work and author.

Here's another situation where an action is illegal, but still ethical. In Civil Disobedience by Thoreau (1846), he states, "If the law is wrong then break it." Based upon this belief, millions of people in the US over the last few decades have demonstrated and protested against various issues. At some point the police have intervened and told them to leave or risk being arrested. Many people chose to break the law and get arrested because they believed so strongly that the law was wrong.

Now, let's bring this into the business world. A large company has a serious management problem. The workers organize a rally and protest outside on the grounds of the business. The workers believe they aren't being treated fairly. They've tried talking with Management but get nowhere. So, they hold this rally and the Company calls the police to disperse the crowd. Several hundred workers refuse to leave. The police give them one final warning then start dispersing the crowd and arresting people. The rally was illegal and the workers failed to move when ordered to do so by the police. The workers did break the law, but were their actions ethical? Thoreau would say, YES! What do you think?

134

In summary, ethics play an important role in the decisions and actions we take. There are several tests that can be used to help sort out one's values and ethics and decide upon the correct form of action. These tests include:

- Role Exchange Test
- Universal Consequences Test
- New Cases Test
- Higher Principles Test

Critical thinking skills such as frames of reference, methodological believing, asking questions and metacognition are useful, if not required when using these tests and attempting to solve an ethical dilemma. When one makes a decision that goes against one's values or ethics, usually there is a consequence. For most people that consequence is an ill feeling such as guilt, regret, uneasiness, anxiety or some other unpleasant (distressed) emotional state. Distress, which has been discussed earlier (see Chapter 7), negatively impacts upon one's thinking and actions.

Summary

- Ethics concerns what we believe to be right and are sometimes referred to as morals.
- Most businesses subscribe to a certain set of ethics
- Oftentimes, critical thinking is needed to sort out various types of ethical dilemmas.
- There are various tests that can be used to help sort out one's values and ethics. Such tests include the Role Exchange Test, the

Universal Consequences Test, the New Cases Test and the Higher Principles Test.

- When you make a decision that goes against your values or ethics, usually you experience some type of distress.
- Distress negatively impacts upon one's thinking and actions.

Exercises for Ethics

In the following situations, identify which "test" to use and attempt to solve the ethical dilemma:

Co-worker who steals –

Sally got a job in a large office through her friend Phyllis. If it wasn't for Phyllis, Sally would never have gotten this job. Sally has discovered that her friend Phyllis is stealing from the Company.

Salesperson who lies –

Barry is the number one salesperson in his company. He gets all sorts of rewards and is admired by everyone. He even serves as a mentor for inexperienced salespeople. One day Victor, an inexperienced sales person accompanied Barry to watch an expert in action. Victor observed Barry lying repeatedly to the customer about the product and the Company's service plan.

Additional Ethical Decision Making Exercises

For each scenario, use one or more of the Ethical Tests to determine the ethical dilemma

1. Dan owns a "green company" – a cleaning company that uses cleaning products that do not harm the environment. Dan has taken some of the profits from the Company and invested in some Mutual Funds. Some of the companies within the Mutual Fund produce products that are toxic and harmful to both people and the environment. Dan justifies this as a "temporary" action to help his company grow and gain more capital.

2. Sharon worked for an educational training company. One day she received an email to her personal email account with a copy of everyone's personal email account included in the letter that had been sent by her supervisor. She never deleted that email. Now she's with a new Company selling educational materials and wants to use that email as a prospective list.

3. Susan is on the hiring committee to select a new CEO for the Company. She knows one candidate very well because he was her former boyfriend. During the time she was in a relationship with him, he told her about some business deals he had made that were clearly unethical and might even have been illegal.

Susan would like to disclose this information to the rest of the committee, but doesn't want to disclose about the relationship she had with him. Based upon the ethical tests, what should she do?

4. David works for a company that is about to begin production on a new tool. All of the tests and assessments of this new tool have been favorable. However, David witnessed one of the tests where the tool clearly failed and it broke. The flaw in this tool has not been corrected. But David's foreman told David, *You didn't seen no*thing. *If you value your job, you will say nothing about this.* David's boss, the foreman, has lots of connections with the higher ups in the company. If you were David, what would you do? What *tests* would you use to determine your decision?

5. Ralph is a newly hired employee who got a job as an oil burner technician. His job is to service oil burners in people's homes. The first few days he is assigned to Steve, a veteran worker to "show him the ropes". Steve teaches Ralph how to do less work and get paid for it. Specifically, they take long coffee breaks between jobs and later take a 2 hour lunch. Steve shows Ralph how he leaves the time blank on the customer's invoice copy, then changes it for the Company's copy. He ends up servicing only four out of six service calls.

Before leaving for the day, Steve senses Ralph is uneasy with what he's doing. He tells him, "look, why work harder than you need to". He also says, "Ya know, I have to evaluate you on how you do with me. You want a good evaluation don't ya? Ya know, you're on probation. So just keep this confidential if you want your job". If you were Ralph, what would you do and what test(s) would you use to determine what to do?

Critical Thinking and Social Media

Most businesses can benefit from some type of Social Media. But the questions is—which one? Social Media if used correctly, can be a real asset to a business. However, if misused, it can be worse than not using it at all. A bad response that goes viral (spreads rapidly like a virus over the Web) can severely hurt a business and even put that business out of business.

To use Social Media properly requires a strategy and a policy. The strategy provides a road map to get from point A to point B. The nature of your business will help you determine which form of Social Media to use. You may decide to use more than one, but it is recommended that you begin with just one platform. You can always add additional ones.

While Facebook is the largest and most popular Social Media platform, is certainly isn't the only one. If you're a graphic artist you might wish to consider Pinterest, which allows you to post pictures and graphics. Deciding which Social Media platform to use is an important decision and is part of your strategy.

Many business owners jump into a social media platform such as Facebook, without giving it much thought. This is a big mistake. You need to take time to decide which platform will benefit your business the most. Even if you have already chosen a platform and are already using Social Media, it would be time well spent to think about your strategy of what you want to do and why you chose the particular form of Social Media that you are using. Many business owners rationalize that since most businesses are already using Social Media, particularly Facebook and Twitter, they should use them as well. It really depends upon the nature of your business.

Twitter works quite differently from Facebook. With Twitter you can send a limited text message as well as follow experts in your field and hopefully get customers to follow you. There is a different strategy used for Twitter than Facebook. So it requires thinking about what would be best for your business. Even if you already are using a particular form of social media, you need to find out if it is worth the effort and producing satisfactory results

When developing or reviewing a strategy, you need to think critically. Specifically that means looking for and challenging assumptions, examining your frames of reference and those of your customers and suppliers. You will probably want to ask yourself several critical thinking questions and think about your own thinking (Metacognition). In some instances you might want to look and see if there is a causal relationship between two different events such as a promotion you ran and the amount of sales that resulted from it.

There are numerous opportunities to use critical thinking. Business owners who don't bother to think critically are the ones that often get into trouble. When you are "transparent" and on the Web, your actions can be viewed very quickly by millions of people. While critical thinking is no guarantee that you will be successful and avoid getting into trouble, it certainly reduces the odds of that happening.

Your strategy is likely to be greatly influenced by your own Frames of Reference and Assumptions. You might also wish to look at Cause and Effect. Will having an account on Twitter actually drive traffic to your business and increase revenue for you? You will need to do some Metacognition and check out any assumptions that you have as well as particular frames of reference. You are also likely to benefit by using Methodological Believing. Adopting the viewpoint of one of your potential customers to try and understand why they would or would not use a particular social media site to learn about your company or to discover it while visiting that site.

Virtually all the critical thinking skills in this book could be used to help you create your strategy. Think critically and carefully before you invest your time (and your money if you are hiring someone to manage your social media marketing). A well thought out strategy can be incredibly useful. But one put together haphazardly can have poor or even harmful results.

Let me share with you one of my experiences with a company that shall remain nameless. Over the course of several months I had seen advertisements in a circular about men's shoes being on sale. Yet, each time I was in the store they didn't have the shoes on sale for the price stated in their publication. The third time this happened I decided to contact the Customer Service Dept online. This action opened up a flurry of emails back and forth. Either they didn't really read my emails or they sent me an auto-responder, because they never addressed the issue and kept talking about buying shoes online. I repeatedly told them that this was an in person transaction.

Finally, I got so exasperated that I sent them one final email telling them that I was going to post this on their website unless they could resolve this issue. They basically said that they didn't care. So I did! When I went to their website, I was shocked to see so many negative comments and I mean really negative comments! I added mine to an ongoing list of complaints, some of which were really nasty.

This is an example of how not to use social media. This particular company doesn't understand why it is called 'social media'. It's not surprising that they are not doing well as a business. If you ignore customers, whether in person or online, you pay a price – a huge price. You can get a negative reputation in a matter of hours.

Some businesses for this reason, have decided not to use social media. However, this is the 21 century and the ways of doing business have changed. When you see major companies, Forture 500 companies and names of companies that you do business with along with other well recognized companies using social media sites, you know it is no longer a passing fad.

Using this media correctly can be a tremendous boost to your company. Using it wrong can be worse than not using it at all.

In addition to a strategy, you also need a policy. Your policy pertains to how you will handle various types of situations.

These include such scenarios as:

- A negative comment placed on your post
- The person managing your social media either quits or is fired.
- Do you allow employees to post comments about your business on your social media site(s) and what happens if they post a negative comment?
- Do you allow employees to post comments about staff meetings and make them public? How transparent do you want/claim to be?
- How quickly do you respond to posts?

These are only a few of some policy decisions that you must make. Your policy should reflect the values of your Company and it's mission statement if you have one. (You don't have a mission statement? You didn't write a business plan? You don't have a marketing plan, except for Social Media? If you said, "No" to any of these questions you are really doing yourself and your business a disservice and really need to go back do your homework.

Is it possible to successfully run a business without doing all this? Maybe, but chances are you will fail. Most businesses do within the first three years.

There's a reason why Social Media is called "social". Some businesses fail to understand this. Before you start to go online and become "social" with your customers and potential customers, get your business in order.

Critical Thinking requires mental effort. A situation usually isn't a simple as it first appears. When you're running a business, you can't afford to skimp on planning and organizing and a great deal of critical thinking is required to do this and to be successful.

Many of the same critical thinking skills you'll use for developing your strategy will also be used for developing your policy. Again, you will need to identify and challenge assumptions, recognize your frame of reference and those of your employees and customers. You will benefit from thinking about your thinking (metacognition) and asking yourself and other critical thinking questions. You may also benefit by using Methodological Believing to gain a better understanding of someone who has an adversary view.

The business world is more competitive than ever. Most business owners realize that everything else being equal – service is what makes the difference. How do you provide better service? Traditionally, you study your competition. You can still do that. However, using various critical thinking skills will help give you the competitive edge. Nearly everyone knows to "check out the competition". But not everyone knows how to think critically. By doing so, you will have a definite advantage which can translate into more sales and raise your bottom line while providing customers with an excellent experience when they buy something at your business, whether it be a service or a product. Some business owners fail to understand this. They don't last long.

Social Media can be a tremendous asset to your business. But, if used improperly, it can be worse than not using it all. You've got to think critically before you do something on the Web, because whatever you do has the potential of going viral.

Strategy – What do you want to accomplish?

As stated above, a strategy is designed to get you from point A to point B. One of the first decisions you will need to make is what social media platform to use. You can begin to immediately use several of the critical thinking skills described in this book.

Assumptions

Are you making any assumptions? Suppose you decided to use Facebook. Be sure that you aren't assuming anything and if you are, try and determine if your assumptions have any real basis. Facebook does offer tremendous opportunity for marketing. But, is Facebook appropriate for your type of business?

While most social media is free, it isn't free in terms of time. It will cost you time to develop and manage a social media platform. If you are a sole-proprietor, will you have time to do this and run the rest of your business? Are you assuming that you will have time to do this? Or, are you assuming that social media will increase your sales to such a degree that you will be able to hire someone to manage your social media account(s).

Millions of people are on Facebook and seem to figure out how to use it. What about you? Are you assuming that you can do it without difficulty? While there are millions of people using this form of social media, remember that Facebook wasn't initially designed for businesses and lots of people who are using Facebook are not business people and don't have a business page.

At this point you may be thinking that I've gone negative about Facebook. I have not! I'm merely trying to point out some assumptions that people have. If you're going to invest your time in using any social media platform, you've got to be able to identify your assumptions and "challenge" them – check them out and determine if what you assume is true or not.

Frames of Reference

You might think the best way to do this is ask some other business owners what they think about social media, and the specific form you are considering, whether it be Facebook, Twitter, Pinterest, Google Plus, just to name a few of them.

Be careful when asking other business owners about their experience and what they think. It will be based upon their "frames of reference". Whether it's

148

good or bad, you'll hear about it if you ask them. Some people will tell you it's a bunch of hype, while others will tell you there is a fantastic opportunity to market your business. Many will fall somewhere in the middle of the two. Both your frame of reference and theirs can influence your decision.

If you ask someone who uses social media for non-business purposes, they will have a different perspective about it. It's important to identify all the various frames of references and realize how they influence people;s decision making and yours as well.

You might be thinking that this is getting to be too complex. Remember that critical thinking frequently deals with complexities and something which initially seems simple often looks much more complex when critical thinking is applied.

The key to developing your strategy is to determine which social media platform will work best for your business. You may find that more than one will serve you well. Before you make your decision, you need to identify any assumptions you are making and carefully check out various frames of reference.

Policy

Once you've decided upon your strategy you will need to develop a policy – whether you are a sole proprietor or work for a medium or larger company. Earlier, I listed a few issues that require some type of policy.

A negative comment placed on your post

Most companies have developed a policy about what to do about this. Many companies will allow a negative comment, as long as it doesn't contain profane words and isn't a complete lie. But some companies do remove negative comments. Those that do are quickly accused of censorship.

Successful companies immediately contact the individual who posted the negative comment and try to resolve the issue. Many customers as so grateful when a representative of a company contacts them in a sincere attempt to resolve the conflict and make the customer happy, that they write a very positive post updating their most recent experience with the company.

As you can see, there are a lot of decisions to be made and it's more efficient to have a policy in place rather than try to deal with these issues as they occur. One critical thinking skill that can really be useful to gain an understanding of why someone would post a negative comment is Methodological Believing. While it may be easy to understand a customer's viewpoint, it's another matter making internal changes in your business to prevent this from happening again. The thing that some businesses don't understand is there is a reason why it is called "social media". You are attempting to develop a relationship with your customers and potential customers.

The worst thing you can do is allow people to post negative comments about your company and not respond to them Yet, there are companies that do this! It's not surprising that those companies are in trouble and their revenue is going down. These companies fail to understand the true nature of "social media" and actually do more harm to themselves than good, by using social media incorrectly.

The person managing your social media either quits or is fired.

To deal with this situation, you will need to check out your assumptions, frames of reference, asking Critical Thinking Questions and even use metacognition. There are all sorts of issues here. Who else has the password to the account? Who else know how to use the account? Where is the password stored, if it is stored? Again, if you have a policy in place, it helps you to deal with a crisis and even prevent one. Suppose you are a sole proprietor and hire someone part time to manage your social media. You're busy running your business and don't have time to learn some software package, so you leave all the responsibility to this person you hired to run your social media programs. Then, that person either leaves or is fired. Now what happens? If you've thought about this using critical thinking, you'll have a policy in place. If you have to re-invent the wheel, it could take a lot of time and be costly, much like what I've been saying about assumptions – they can be "costly and dangerous".

Do you allow employees to post comments about your business on your social media site(s) and what happens if they post a negative comment?

This is a policy decision that relates to internal structure and how you run your business (Mission Statement). Something is wrong if an employee feels the only way he or she can reach the company is by posting a negative comment about the company. There needs to be someone that an employee can speak with if they have an issue with the company. For someone to have to resort to posting a negative comment on the company's post clearly indicates there is a communication problem and even more with this company. There are numerous critical thinking questions that need to be asked by the people running this company.

Do you allow employees to post comments about staff meetings and make them public? How transparent do you want/claim to be?

Many companies bulk at this and feel it's a breach of confidentiality. But other companies that really aspire to be transparent have a different view. Whatever your company decides, there are a number of critical thinking skills to use to deal with this issue, including: Asking Critical Thinking Questions, Assumptions, Frames of Reference Cause and Effect, Metacognition and possibly Ethical Reasoning.

How quickly do you respond to posts?

The answer to this question might seem obvious —as quickly as possible. However, if you're a sole proprietor, you may not be able to respond as quickly as you would like to respond. Once again, there are a number of critical thinking skills to consider, including Asking Critical Thinking Questions, Identifying and Challenging Assumptions, Frames of Reference, Metacognition, and Cause and Effect.

As you can see, there are many decisions to make that require some critical thinking skills. Create your strategy and develop your policy in advance. If you wait until you have a crisis, you will be under pressure to take action and might take the wrong action. Whatever you do could possibly be viewed by millions of people depending upon how active you are in social media and how many people are following you - either on Facebook, Twitter, Pinterest or some other social media site such as Google +, LinkedIn, just to name a few of them.

There are a number of books and web articles that will provide you with technical information on how to use various social media platforms. This book focuses upon various critical thinking skills to use when selecting what platforms to use (strategy) and what to do with each social media site (policy). There are numerous decisions to make and it becomes an on-going process. However, proper planning will help you avert a crisis. Once you have a strategy and policy in place you'll have a good foundation. This certainly doesn't mean that a new issue won't arise. It will! But, you will hopefully have a good frame of reference to use to solve new issues. If, however, you wait until you have a crisis because you have given this little or no thought and certainly haven't used critical thinking, you're likely to have a crisis and have it last longer.

Remember, that events can happen very quickly and news of your problem can spread like a virus and go 'virual'. Some businesses have really paid the price by not thinking critically in this respect. While you can never fully protect yourself against a negative comment or some other type of crisis, you can prevent the likelihood of some type of crisis by thinking critically about your strategy and your policy. Your policy will probably reflect the values of your company. Values are important and good companies have integrity and are consistent in how they conduct business. These types of issues often require some ethical reasoning and a good deal of thought.

While this book is applicable to any size business, it may be of greater value to the sole proprietor who overnight decides to jump on the social media band wagon. If you are the only one running your business, you must think really carefully about the various actions you want to take. It requires a lot more time than it takes to get an account and get a presence on social media.

Even setting up an account on a social media platform can require some critical thinking. Just how public and visible to you want to be? There are a number of settings, particularly on Facebook that really require some thought. So, before you go clicking on various permissions and settings, do some metacognition and ask yourself some critical thinking questions. Many of these questions involve 'cause and effect'. Ask your self such questions as, "If I allow this setting what could be the effect?" Do you really want the world to have your personal phone number and address where you live? While such a question seems obvious, there are other settings that require much more thought.

In summary,

Using social media requires a considerable amount of critical thinking skills. You'll need to first have a strategy and then a policy. As you continue to use various social media, there will be decisions you will need to make. If you succeed in developing a good following of customers and potential customers, remember that they are watching your sites. This makes it all the more important to think critically before you act. Use any of the following critical thinking skills to help you run a successful social media campaign.

Assumptions—look for assumptions and challenge them. When you are creating your strategy, identify and challenge any assumptions you have. Continue to do this as you set your policy. As you develop your presence on social media platforms, continue to look for assumptions – yours and those of others.

Frames of Reference—are usually based upon experiences either good or bad. Keep this in mind when you ask people, particularly other business owners about their thoughts and feelings on social media, Remember to check your own frames of reference, which can greatly influence your decisions.

Critical Thinking Questions—Whether your creating a strategy or policy or challenging an assumption, you will need to ask yourself and others various critical thinking questions. Recall that there are various types of questions you can ask to gather information, seek evidence, challenge assumptions and frames of reference, probe for consequences (cause and effect), and question your own thinking as well as question other people's questions.

Metacognition—Thinking about one's thinking. You will certainly want think about your own thinking and look for flaws in your logic, assumptions, frames of reference and ask yourself several critical thinking questions.

Methodological Believing—this special type of role play can help you to understand an opposing point of view. It can valuable to help you understand your customers, your employees and even policies and events that you might initially automatically oppose.

Cause and Effect—you will undoubtedly want to use this critical thinking skill to see if what you are planning to do will produce positive results. From your strategy to policy to on-going business affair, be on the lookout for cause and effect relationships and recognize that you may need other critical thinking skills to really determine if there is a cause and effect relationship or not.

Ethical Reasoning—As long as you're in business, from time to time there will be ethical issues that arise. Use the various critical thinking ethical tests to help you arrive a decision that you believe is 'right'.

As discussed, there are many ethical issues that can arise in social media. Use these tests as tools to help you decide your correct response.

Stress Management—While this is not a critical thinking skill, recall that stress management can be used to promote critical thinking. When you are stressed is the worst time to make a decision. Lower your stress level using the Recent Pleasant Experience and the on-going Inventory and Journal to deal with harsh criticism and your own self criticism. Remember, when you use social media you are public. Think (critically) before you act.

Exercises

List some assumptions you have about social media. Example: Social media is more hype than anything else.

1.

2.

3.

Ask yourself some critical thinking questions. Example: How do I know this is true. How could I find out? What evidence do I need and how could I get such evidence?

1.

2.

3.

Identify your Frames of Reference concerning thoughts/assumptions regarding social media.. Example: My friends all are very positive about social media. Business owners I contacted had mixed feelings about social media.

1.

2.

3.

Select one form of social media that you wish to use.

- Make a list of all the reasons for using this particular social media platform
- What specifically do you hope to accomplish?
- How will you accomplish this? What is your plan?
- How will you know when you've accomplished your goal?
- Will you manage the social media platform yourself or will you have someone else do it?. Will you have the time to do it yourself? Ap-

proximately, how much time do you think it
will take .If you hire someone else to do it,
who will you hire and how will you select
them?

- Have you thought of any of these questions
before reading them? If "yes", that's great!
If "no", then you need to go back and read
about developing your plan and then work
on developing it. Ask yourself lots of critical
thinking questions.

Using Critical Thinking in Your Social Media Selection.

List some critical thinking skills you might use in
selecting your social media platform. Provide a reason
for using this particulat critical thinking skill.

1.

2.

3.

Critical Thinking in Business

In today's competitive business world, businesses must have an edge to remain competitive and be successful. That edge can be employing people who can think critically. It's not enough to hire someone with an MBA. That person needs to have critical thinking skills.

In previous chapters I've described a number of critical thinking skills and explained how those skills can be using in business. These skills, like any skill, need to be practiced. The good news is that you can practice them in your own person life in addition to the workplace. While I've emphasized using various critical thinking skills at work, the fact is these skills can be used in your personal life as well. Here is a review of those skills.

ASSUMPTIONS

An engineering firm would never just design a bridge and assume the design would work. They'd test it out based upon mathematical formulas, laws of physics and engineering concepts. Basing an idea or design for a bridge on merely an assumption could be disastrous.

In the business world, assumptions can be dangerous and costly as well. Each day people working in the business world have decisions to make, proposals to evaluate and various actions to take. Assumptions need to be identified and challenged to determine if there is any truth or not to what is being assumed. Critical thinkers just don't assume whatever they hear or read about to be true. They seek evidence and challenge assumptions.

ASKING CRITICAL THINKING QUESTIONS

One of the ways assumptions can be challenged is by asking questions. As discussed previously, there are several different sets of questions that you can ask. Some of those categories include asking questions that clarify, seek evidence and even asking questions about questions. You can gain information by asking questions. You can also encourage people to think critically by asking them questions which require them to give some type of proof or evidence for whatever they are claiming.

FRAMES OF REFERENCE

Marketing and salespeople recognized the value in identifying a customer's frame of reference or perspective. Frames of reference can play an important role in marketing. In addition, negotiations of business contracts can be aided by an understanding of the other party's frame of reference. Sometimes sales are lost, contracts are stalled or lost, negotiations break down because people fail to understand another person's frame of reference. Understanding and recognizing frames of reference is a valuable critical thinking skill. It's also helpful to recognize your own personal frames of reference.

METHODOLOGICAL BELIEVING

Methodological Believing is a unique role play that provides you with a greater understanding of an opposing point of view, including other people's frames of reference. This is a skill that really needs to be developed by practicing. It's best to start with a fairly neutral issue and gradually progress to more polarized issues. Using this technique you adopt the opposing point of view and vigorously support it and defend it for a short duration of about 5 minutes or less. This is an excellent way to gain some understanding about an opposing point of view.

CAUSAL REASONING

This is a type of logic that attempts to establish a cause and effect relationship between two unrelated things. As discussed in a previous chapter, a manager thought there was a cause and effect relationship between a sales slump in August and the extremely hot and humid weather. However, cause and effect relationships can be deceiving and in this case the causal relationship was proven to be false. Oftentimes other critical thinking skills are needed to analyze a situation and determine if there really is a causal relationship or not. Seeking evidence and challenging assumptions are some of those skills that are needed.

METACOGNITION

Thinking about one's thinking (metacognition) is a critical thinking skill that includes many other critical thinking skills as well. When you begin to think about your thinking, you will begin to identify some assumptions you have made. You'll discover your frames of reference. You may be able to detect flaws in your thinking. This is a critical thinking skill that is useful for anyone in business, regardless of what position you hold. It is a very useful and important critical thinking skill.

ETHICS

Business ethics are important and there are several "tests" to help you determine your values and ethics as was discussed in a previous chapter. Unethical business behavior may not be illegal. But, while you may not end up in court with a lawsuit, you may find the court of public opinion to be unforgiving. Customers who perceive that a business isn't treating them fairly or is cheating them in some manner will naturally boycott that business. You may find yourself in a difficult dilemma concerning ethics that will require you to either use one of the "tests" discussed earlier or use some other critical thinking skills to decide what to do.

There are many other critical thinking skills. In addition, the role that stress plays in critical thinking can not be underestimated. Recall that too much stress turns into distress and makes critical thinking impossible. While stress management in itself is not a critical thinking skill, it does help to promote critical thinking.

Critical thinking is a set of thinking skills that can be used in practically any aspect of business. CEOs of large and middle size companies and even sole proprietors can use critical thinking to help their businesses remain competitive and successful. Managers, marketing people, people in sales, finance, human resources and those people involved in accounting and payroll can all benefit by using various critical thinking skills.

If you're a sole proprietor, you must make all the decisions for your business. It is imperative that you use critical thinking.

Here again is a list of the various critical thinking skills that have been discussed in this book. Apply them to your business and keep practicing them. Like any other skill, the more your practice and use them, the more skilled you will become.

The Skills:

Asking Critical Thinking Questions—a variety of questions to ask to gain more information, clarity, evidence, challenge assumptions and examining consequences

Identifying and Challenging Assumptions—look for anything you take for granted or that hasn't been proven and "challenge it". Determine if it true or not.

Frames of Reference—perspectives or viewpoints can greatly influence your decision making. A frame of reference can turn into an assumption. Besides your own frame of reference, other people have their own frames of reference as well.

Methodological Believing—a special type of role play where you adopt an opposing point of view and vigorously support it for a few minutes to gain an understanding of such a view.

Causal Reasoning—an attempt to determine if one event causes another. This skill is best used with other critical thinking skills, rather than by itself.

Metacognition—Thinking about one's thinking. Examining your own thoughts for flaws in logic, assumptions and frames of reference. Asking yourself a number of questions.

Ethical Reasoning—determing what is 'right' or 'wrong' based upon four different ethical tests. Ethical reasoning frequently draws upon many other critical thinking skills previous discussed.

Stress Management—recall that Stress Management is not a critical thinking skill, but can be used to promote critical thinking. The best time to make a decision is when you are relaxed and not stressed.

To Do:

On a separate piece of paper, make a list of all the critical thinking skills you recall after reading this book. Provide a brief definition for each skill. Practice applying these skills into your work setting each day.

Conclusion

As I have demonstrated throughout this book, critical thinking skills are practical skills that can be used right in the workplace – right on the job. Those businesses that wish to get ahead, to remain above the competition, will employ people that have critical thinking abilities.

Bob Schoenberg

You can email Bob at: Bobsch3@gmail.com

Bibliography

R.J. Banis (Ed.) 2001 .Copyright Issues for Librarians, Teachers & Authors–2nd Edn (2001) Chesterfield MO Science & Humanities Press

Beyer 1988. Developing a Thinking Skills Program. Boston, MA: Allyn and Bacon, Inc.

Bradford, J. A. 1994. "Suspending Judgement, Using Critical Thinking in Business" N.E. Nonprofit Quarterly. Fall 1994

Braun, N.A. "Critical Thinking in the Business Curriculum. Journal of Education for Business. March-April 2004 v79 i4 p232(5).

Browne, N.M. and S. Keeley. 2001 Asking the right Questions: A Guilde to Critcial Thinking. 6th Edition. Upper Saddle River, NJ: Prentice-Hall.

Diestler, S. 2001. Becoming a Critical Thinker A User Friendly Manual. 3rd Edition, Upper Saddle River, NJ. Prentice-Hall, Inc.

Drucker, P. F. "Theory of Business", Harvard Business Review. Sept.-Oct. 1994 v. 72 n5 pp. 95 (10).

Elbow, P. 1986. "Methodological Doubt and Believing Contraries in Inquiry". Embracing Contraries. NY: Oxford University Press.

Ennis in Fischer, A. PDF File (http://austhink.org/critical/pages/definitions.html).

Fischer and Schriven 1997. pp.21 in (http://austhink.org/critical/pages/definitions.html)

Gelder, T.V. (http://austhink.org/critical/pages/definitions.html).

Hall, M.L. <u>Reframing for Creatively New Managing Options</u> (http://www.neurosemantics.com/Articles/Manage ment-by-Reframing.htm)

Janis, I.I. 1982. "Decision Making Under Stress". <u>Handbook of Stress Theoretical and Clinical Aspects</u>. NY: Free Press.

Klar, Blar-Tal & Kruglanski. 1987. "Conflict Frames of Reference: Implications for Dispute Process and Outcomes". <u>Academy of Management Journal</u>. Vol. 37. No. 1. Feb. 1994 pp. 193-205.

Lee, S.P. 2002. <u>What is the Argument?</u>, Boston, MA: McGraw-Hill Companies, Inc.

Mandler, G. 1982. "Stress and Thought Processes". <u>Handbook of Stress Theoretical and Clinical Aspects</u>. NY: Free Press.

Meichenbaum, D. 1983. <u>Coping with Stress</u>. NY: Fact on File Publication.

Montana, P.J. and B. Charnov. "Linear Thinking". <u>Management</u>. 2000. Barons Educational Series, Inc.

Nagle, R.J. and G. Smith. 1995. "Frames of Reference and Buyer's Perception of Price and Value". California Management Review. Fall.

Nickerson, Perkins and Smith 1985. in (http://austhink.org/critical/pages/definitions.html)

Paul, R. 1990. Critical Thinking. Rohnert Park: Sonoma State University.

Paul, R. and S. Elder. 2001. CRITICAL THINK-ING Tools for Taking Charge of Your Learning and Your Life. Upper Saddle River, NJ: Prentice-Hall.

Pinkly and Northcraft 1994. "Conflict Frames of Reference: Implications for Dispute Processes and Outcomes". Academy of Management Journal.

Sargent, T. 1984. The Behavioral and Medical Efffects of Stress. Hartford CT: Designed Change Institute Publications.

Seyle, H. 1974. Stress Without Distress. Phila-delphia, PA: J.P. Lippincott Company.

Shapiro, A. TEACHING CRITICAL THINK-ING: The Believing Game & the Doubting Game. (http://www.teachablemoment.org/high/critical thinking.html).

Swartz R.J. and D.N. Perkins. 1990. Teaching Thinking: Issues & Approaches. Pacific Grove, CA: Midwest Publications.

Teays, W., 2003. Second Thoughts Critical Thinking for a Diverse Society. Boston, MA: McGraw-Hill Companies, Inc.

Wolff, M.A. 1986. "According to Whom? Helping Students Analyze, Contrasting View of Reality". Educational Leadership. October Issue. pp. 36-41.

Appendix

Suggested Answers to Exercises
Statements true (T) of false (F)

1. F
2. T
3. F
4. T
5. T
6. F
7. F
8. F
9. T
10. F

Chapter Two – Assumptions

1. Assumption – Because sales were good last month doesn't necessarily mean they will be good next month.
2. Assumption – The statement is speculative or merely an opinion.
3. Fact
4. Assumption – Not even meteorologists are certain what the weather will be.
5. Assumption. This statement could be true if additional information was provided. It is

also possible that an improvement could be made by changing procedures.

6. Assumption – Unfortunately, this isn't always true.
7. Fact
8. Assumption – There is no evidence within this statement to support it.
9. Assumption – An increase in marketing will not necessarily result in more sales.
10. Assumption – There is no evidence given to support this statement. No company could continue to do poor work. They would go out of business.
11. Assumption – Unless all factory workers took an IQ test and scored poorly the author of this statement would have no idea of how bright a worker is. In addition, the author would need to document a correlation between intelligence and creativity.
12. Assumption – not all traveling routes are the same.
13. Fact
14. Assumption
15. Assumption
16. Assumption
17. Assumption
18. Fact
19. Assumption
20. Assumption – Unless this is stated in the Employee manual, it is not known if that employee will be fired.
21. Fact – However, this doesn't guarantee that there will be a party this year.
22. Assunption

23. Fact
24. Fact
25. Assumption
26. Assumption
27. Assumption
28. Assumption
29. Fact
30. Assumption (This is a very common assumption made in marketing)
31. I'm in a hurry to make some copies. The copier will probably jam.

Chapter Three - Asking Questions

There are numerous possible answers. There is no one, specific answer.

Chapter Four – Frames of Reference.

For these exercises, there is no one single correct answer. Answers provided are suggestions. Your answers may differ. (Note: not all answers are provided to this section due to the wide variation of possible responses).

1. An accountant – numbers
2. A Marketing person – getting the word out
3. Sales person – selling, closing the sale
4. Lawyer – legal
5. CEO – responsibility for business/organization
6. job applicant – getting hired, projecting a good image
7. a Doctor – medical/health

Convenience store – we need this store at this location. How do we convince the neighbors to allow it.? We've successfully negotiated with other neighbors before. Or, we've never been in this situation before. How do we proceed?

IT Specialists – This is better/worse than other products.

Accounting Dept. – We're in trouble. Better make sure everything adds up.

Sales Dept. – We can/can not reach this quota. Or, we'll reach this quota.

Worker injured on the job – I hope my employer will pay my expenses. Employer – we're sorry the worker got injured, but it was his fault, not ours.

Customer with computer problem – this is a waste of my time. I remember the last time I had a computer problem ... .

Identify the business and why you would choose it – for each of these examples, provide a specific business name and a reason for choosing that business – which could be good experience, good reputation, location, price, etc.

Identifying your personal frame of reference
– Answers will vary. Here are some possible answers. (Note, there is no one single correct answer).

1. Bread – gee they raised the price!
2. Annual Review – relating to last year's experience – or if new, apprehension, worry about the Review.
3. Meet with boss, now! Worry, concern you did something wrong.
4. Traffic jam – I knew I should have left earlier. Or, I should have taken an alternative route. Or, I'd better call in and let them know I'm going to be late. Or, not again! I could be fired for being late this time!
5. We worked hard to get this. It's great to be recognized.
6. Pink slip – I hope I don't get one
7. New hired employee - The new guy seems very competent/incompetent
8. Computer File – Where is that file? Have I been hacked? Did I save it?
9. Lunch invitation – I don't like this place. What excuse do I make?
10. Project – I've got to find out how to do this. Or, oh no, I haven't a clue how to do this. How am I'm going to do it?
11. New Supervisor - (many possible responses). Good riddance! What is the new Supervisor going to be like? Gee, I will miss my current supervisor.

Christmas bonus – I think they made a mistake. Should I speak up? Or, I am definitely going to inquire about this.

12. Central Supply room – Not my business! Or, this is wrong. I need to do something about this.

13. Missing pen – Where's my pen? Did someone take it? Did I misplace it. Do we have a thief working here?

14. Training program ½ day. Another waste of time! Or, oh good, a training program. I can learn something new and get a break from work.

Outdoor barbeque scenario

Fireman – Is that fire under control?

Young man just returning from the gym. – I'm hungry, When are we going to eat? Will there be enough food?

Vegetarian – Hope they have something other than meat.

CH Five - Methodological Believing

Exercise #1 - Time Card Issue

For this exercise, adopt the opposite point of view and argue passionately for as many reasons as possible supporting this point of view. Do this for 2-5 minutes and write down your answers on paper.

Exercise #2 – Social Media

Support the opposite point of view and list as many reasons as you can think of and write them down. Argue passionately for this position. Spend 2-5 minutes doing this and write down your reasons on a piece of paper.

Exercise #3 – Return Policy

Adopt the opposite point of view and argue passionately for that position. Write your reasons down on paper. Spend 2-5 minutes doing this.

Exercise #4 Personal Internet Use at Work

Adopt the opposite point of view and argue passionately for it. Write your arguments down on paper and do this for 2-5 minutes.

Exercise #5 Sale Price

Adopt the opposite point of view and argue passionately for it. Write your argument on paper and do this for 2-5 minutes.

CH Six – Cause and Effect

1. yes
2. no – although the audience thought that it was the plant causing the problem
3. no
4. no
5. yes
6. no (The real cause is improper placement of the finger over the hole).
7. no
8. yes
9. no
10. yes
11. yes
12. yes
13. no
14. yes
15. yes
16. no
17. yes
18. yes
19. yes
20. no

Metacognition

1. Crossing the river. In solving this problem, look for assumptions, frames of reference, and flaws in your thinking. Notice any patterns or particular strategy you used in at-

tempting to solve this problem. Were they helpful or a hinderance?

Actual answer. The man takes the chicken in his boat and travels across the river, leaving the chicken on the bank of the river. He then goes back and takes the dog across the river, where he puts the chicken back into his boat. He goes back and gets the grain, leaving the dog. He takes the grain across the river to the chicken, where he puts the chicken in the boat and returns to the dog. He puts the dog in the boat and goes across the river, leaving the dog with the bag of grain. He goes back and gets the chicken and goes across the river and now has successfully transported all three items. (There many be other ways of doing this).

Copy and Paste Exercise

Focus on how you attempted to solve the problem, identifying frames of references, assumptions, patterns and strategies. Note if any of these were helpful or not.

Answer – the cursor must be repositioned. You can not go where you haven't already typed. So, you must "force the cursor" by pressing the ENTER key and re-position the cursor.

Rectangle Problem

Focus on how you attempted to solve the problem, identifying frames of reference, assumptions, patterns and strategies. Note if any were helpful or a hindrance. Also look for flaws in your thinking.

Answer: Remove the 2nd line that goes across in each column

Answer: Remove all interior lines in the first two column

Team Building Exercise

Try this one with a group of people. Focus on your frames of reference, identify assumptions, loot for patterns and strategies that you have used in the past. Look for flaws in your thinking.

Answer: Each person must have their hand on the "pass" (even a finger will suffice).

CH Nine – Ethical Reasoning

The "correct" answer to any of these dilemmas depends upon your values. Your values and the actions you take must be consistent. What is important to you is what you value. Use the four Ethical Reasoning Tests to determine your "correct" answer.

Example, for the Green Company, if Dan values making money more than helping the environment, then, for him, investing in a company that makes a toxic product is consistent with his value of making money – which he places higher than keeping the planet "green". Conversely, if he really values protecting the planet by selling household cleaners that aren't toxic and do not harm the environment, then his actions are not consistent with his values.

Ch 11 Critical Thinking and Social Media

Critical Thinking Skills you might use for selecting your social media platform

1. Identifying and Challenging Assumptions – You might be basing your decision on an assumption.

2. Frames of Reference – you may be influenced by other business owners or friends.

3. Cause and Effect – you might believe that using a particular social media platform will result in significant traffic to your website or store front. This could also be an assumption. The only way to really know for sure is to use that particular social media platform. It will also depend HOW you use it.

About Bob Schoenberg

Bob Schoenberg has a Masters Degree in Critical & Creative Thinking and teaches an online graduate course in Critical Thinking that he created for the University of Massachusetts at Boston. He also conducts training seminars and workshops in southern New England. He is a graduate of the Critical and Creative Thinking Program at UMass, Boston, which is the only school in the country to offer a Masters degree in Critical Thinking.

Prior to teaching Critical Thinking, Mr. Schoenberg served as a software trainer and stress management consultant. He incorporates stress management into his course in Critical Thinking based on the premise that one can't think critically if one is stressed.

Bob has an extensive background in training and curriculum development. Combining his background as a software trainer, educator and curriculum developer, he provides a comprehensive and highly effective online experience for his students. He brings practical business experience to the online classroom as well with over 12 years experience as an entrepreneur and business owner.

You can reach Bob Schoenberg by email at: bobsch3@gmail.com

Made in the USA
Monee, IL
12 January 2021